ROOTED IN LOVE

Louis and Zélie Martin:
Models of Married Love, Family Life,
and Everyday Holiness

ROOTED IN LOVE

Louis and Zélie Martin:
Models of Married Love, Family Life,
and Everyday Holiness

ANNETTE GOULDEN

ICS Publications
Institute of Carmelite Studies
Washington, D.C.

ICS Publications
2131 Lincoln Road NE
Washington, DC 20002-1199
www.icspublications.org

© Washington Province of Discalced Carmelites, Inc., 2021

Cover and text design and pagination by Rose Design
Printed in the United States of America

Cover image: From the reliquary of Sts. Louis and Zélie Martin, with permission from Sanctuaire Sainte Thérèse de Lisieux- France. Photo by Mercy McNab.

Library of Congress Cataloging-in-Publication Data

Names: Goulden, Annette, author.
Title: Rooted in love : Louis and Zélie Martin: models of married love,
    family life, and everyday holiness / Annette Goulden.
Identifiers: LCCN 2020029032 (print) | LCCN 2020029033 (ebook) | ISBN
    9781939272898 (trade paperback) | ISBN 9781939272904 (ebook)
Subjects: LCSH: Martin, Louis, Saint, 1823-1894. | Martin, Zélie, Saint,
    1831-1877. | Christian saints--Biography. | Marriage--Religious
    aspects--Catholic Church.
Classification: LCC BX4655.3 .G68 2020 (print) | LCC BX4655.3 (ebook) |
    DDC 282.092/2 [B]--dc23
LC record available at https://lccn.loc.gov/2020029032
LC ebook record available at https://lccn.loc.gov/2020029033

ISBN: 978-1-939272-89-8 (pbk)
ISBN: 978-1-939272-90-4 (ebook)

For my husband, Peter, who has been a rock of strength
and support in writing this book; our sons Mike and Nick;
our beautiful daughters-in-law, Louise and Angela;
and our grandchildren, Heath and Pearl.

CONTENTS

Foreword by Cyprian Blamires, O.C.D.S. ix

Preface by Lynn and Tim Bete, O.C.D.S. xiii

Acknowledgments xvii

Abbreviations xix

Introduction 1

1 The Story of a Marriage 9

2 A Man and a Woman of Their Past 19

3 A Time of Upheaval 33

4 An Ideal Marriage? 50

5 Birth and Death, Infancy and Old Age 62

6 Work and Wealth 82

7 Terminal Illness 97

8 The Transforming Experience of Parenting 120

9 A Father's Journey 140

10 Loss of the Mind 161

11 The Spirituality of Marriage 178

12 Gathering Up the Fragments 196

Permissions 203

Bibliography 205

FOREWORD

A WHILE AGO I FOUND myself acting as one of the bearers of a casket containing the relics of a very special married couple newly canonized by the church—Louis and Zélie Martin—as they were carried into Plymouth Cathedral in the county of Devon, UK. It was a long and winding road that had led me to this point in my life, a road whose direction I could never have anticipated in earlier times. Although of course God is at work in our lives in ways unknown to us from our earliest days, I can identify certain crucial points of decision. At seventeen, I made a faith commitment as an Anglican; nearly fifteen years later I took the Catholic plunge and was received into the church. Thirteen years after that I found my way into the Secular Order of Discalced Carmelites (O.C.D.S.), into which I was welcomed by Dr. Annette Goulden, O.C.D.S., author of the present work. Annette was a kind, thoughtful, and very forgiving guide and mentor for me in the ways of Carmel, and I am delighted to be able to repay my debt to her in a small way by commending this present work, the first to come from her pen but I sincerely hope not the last. As a writer myself though, I know it is a demanding and challenging vocation.

When I first met Annette, I knew her as a child and adolescent psychiatrist. After her subsequent retirement she was able to give more of her time and energies to the development of the Carmelite Seculars in England and Wales. The present work arises out of her deep love for the saints of Carmel and out of her deep desire to spread the experience and the joy of Carmel as widely as possible. It is true that neither St. Louis nor St. Zélie were in fact Carmelites, but perhaps we can allow them a kind of honorary Carmelite status in that four of their children entered Carmel, of whom one, St. Thérèse of Lisieux, was to become the most famous Carmelite of modern times.

The elevation of St. Louis and St. Zélie to the altars was a unique event in so many ways. Their daughter Thérèse had already been canonized long before them. Each of them aspired to the religious life, but each was turned away. And they were the very first married couple in all of Catholic history to be canonized together. It is this last fact that lies at the heart of Goulden's book. Her long professional experience in working with the psychology of children and parents, plus her own experience of marriage and of parenting two sons, combine here with her deep love for the Catholic faith and her deep Carmelite insights into the faith to make her an ideal biographer of a most extraordinary family.

Having experienced the transforming power of God in her own life through the church and through Carmel, Goulden is particularly concerned to convey how saints like Louis and Zélie can speak out of their time and across the years to us to help us find the grace we need to live our own lives in our own time, in our families and in our homes, as witnesses to the richness and depth of the divine love for us. She wants us to grasp that the sanctity and glowing example of this special married couple is not something beyond our own reach, for in so many ways they were just like us in their struggles and in the pressures they had to cope with.

By elevating these nineteenth-century saints Louis and Zélie to the altars, the church has provided inspirational models to all couples and families struggling to live out their faith in the circumstances and conditions of the twenty-first century. Their times and the conditions they knew were in many ways much closer to ours than we might think. And that makes the story of this family a wonderful gift to us today.

—CYPRIAN BLAMIRES, O.C.D.S.

PREFACE

WRITING THE PREFACE for a book on the lives of Louis and Zélie Martin seemed like a challenging task until we read Annette Goulden's words early on in *Rooted in Love*: "Louis and Zélie demonstrate that it is with this ordinary stuff of quite unremarkable lives that God longs to transform us into the image of his Son."

Ordinary and unremarkable were things to which we could relate. Zélie loved to shop for her children and our front porch is often littered with Amazon boxes. Louis enjoyed fishing and we built our house because of its proximity to a pond. (Okay, at least one of us was motivated by easy access to the pond.)

There were other similarities between our lives. We've moved several times with the resulting chaos. We've gone on pilgrimages with our daughters. We've enjoyed gardening. (Okay, at least one of us enjoys gardening.) And we've experienced a daughter entering the convent—Dominican, not Carmelite—and may have another daughter entering in the future.

Like Louis and Zélie, we've attempted to embrace the daily experiences of life with a "sense of humor, compassion, and perseverance, all based on a profound trust in God." We found the sense of humor and trust in God to be particularly important after we accidentally forgot to pick up one of our daughters and she waited alone for two hours before we realized our mistake. There was also the time shortly after entering the convent that our daughter Maria, who is a Dominican

Sister, mistook ketchup for French salad dressing and silently ate her "Heinz salad."

What we found exceptional in Goulden's take on Louis and Zélie was her ability to highlight how typical the couple really was in their time—"No one thought the Martin household was particularly exceptional." Their daily struggles balancing work as a watchmaker and lace-maker with raising a family were constant. Their efforts to keep Sunday as family time were ever-present. Extended family and friends were a source of both joy and strife. Their grief at the passing of many of their children was always with them. Yet through it all, a life of prayer, daily Mass, and faith in God abounded. Their persistence is an example for all married couples and families today.

Perhaps the greatest thing Goulden provides is a vision for each of our stages of life. Change is unavoidable. We haven't lost any children but have suffered the pain of a miscarriage. We sat by the bed of a dear friend as he died of ALS (also known as motor neuron disease). Half of our children are out of the nest and the others will be out too soon. We've lost one of our parents and the others are getting older. We're getting older, too.

We see Zélie suffer from cancer and the family attempt to deal with the significant hole her death left among them. In our own lives, we've seen the impact the death of a parent can have on young children, too.

Especially in Louis's life, we see him give over his life to God as a single man, a father, a husband, a single parent, and finally as an elderly man with dementia. We see his daughters go through their own stages of life, with each stage requiring a renewed dedication to the will of God.

While we haven't experienced all of the struggles in Louis and Zélie's lives, their experiences are universal. Who knows the exact reasons God allows such things to enter our lives? The older we get, the greater becomes the mystery—including the mystery of the Sacrament of Marriage so beautifully displayed by Louis and Zélie. Nothing but the Sacrament of Marriage teaches patience, humility, and the mercy of God so quickly and effectively. Sometimes it is like a fine piece of sandpaper, slowly removing our rough edges, and at other times it is like a heavy-duty router, gouging away the parts of our lives that need to be removed to increase virtue. Whether it's our relationship with each other, our children or our extended families, there is a constant call to embrace the Little Way that grew out of seeds planted by Louis and Zélie in the life of St. Thérèse.

Perhaps one of the greatest blessings in our lives is sharing the call to Carmel. Both of us are Secular Carmelites—Lynn joining the Order many years before Tim did. We were particularly touched to learn more about the parents of St. Thérèse, gaining a glimpse into what it must have been like to be a child of Louis and Zélie. There's the old saying that the apple doesn't fall far from the tree, and it was certainly the case with Thérèse and her sisters. It's clear that their strong faith and dedication to our Lord had its foundation in Louis and Zélie.

While we entered Carmel at different times, we're members of the same OCDS Community—an extended spiritual family in which we share similar joys and suffering as in our biological family. In a way, we've been blessed to combine the lives of Louis and Zélie as parents with that of St. Thérèse and her call to Carmel. Not that we live behind cloister walls, although the thought of hours of silence was very appealing when our children were young, loud, and demanding. Rather that, like Louis and Zélie, we're called to balance both apostolic and contemplative lives.

Yet while they provide an example of the road to sanctity, Goulden rightly points out that "We are called to the same level of self-giving as the saint but not to copy the saint." We are not called to be the parents of St. Thérèse and her sisters but rather our own children, in our own time. The work and prayer God calls us to is today, not in the late 1800s. We have to forge our own paths in our own lives, marriages, and families. Thanks to Goulden for using Louis and Zélie Martin to show us that "while big events stand out, it is the small, even hesitant steps of the journey in life that God values and magnifies."

—LYNN BETE, O.C.D.S., AND TIM BETE, O.C.D.S.
Our Mother of Good Counsel Secular Carmelite community,
Dayton, Ohio

Lynn and Tim Bete have been married for 30 years and are parents of four children: Sister Maria Benedicta, O.P., Paul, Annie and Grace. They live outside Dayton, Ohio and served as co-chairs for the 2018 O.C.D.S. Congress. Tim is president of a faith-based affordable housing non-profit and Lynn is president of the Our Mother of Good Counsel Secular Carmelite community, of which they are both members in Dayton, Ohio.

ACKNOWLEDGMENTS

I WOULD LIKE TO THANK the late Father Jimmy McCaffrey, O.C.D., and Joanne Mosley for starting me on this journey of writing a book about Louis and Zélie Martin, and for Joanne's unstinting help and advice when needed. My thanks also go to Patricia Morrison, editorial director of ICS Publications, for her clear and practical guidance along the path of publishing, and to Brother Pier Giorgio Pacelli, O.C.D., managing editor, who cheerfully picked up the reins after Pat's retirement from ICS.

I am deeply grateful to Sister Jo Robson, O.C.D., of Ware Carmel for her rigorous editing and endless patience, stirred with a magnificent sense of humor.

I would also like to thank my family, friends, and secular Carmelites who have encouraged me throughout, especially Caroline, for her enthusiasm and interest as each chapter was born.

ABBREVIATIONS

Sts. Zélie and Louis Martin

All quotations from the letters of Zélie and Louis Martin are taken from *A Call to a Deeper Love: The Family Correspondence of the Parents of Saint Thérèse of the Child Jesus, 1863–1885*, edited by Frances Renda, translated by Ann Connors Hess (New York: Society of St. Paul, 2011).

The abbreviation for this work is as follows:

CF *Correspondance Familiale*

St. Elizabeth of the Trinity

All quotations of Elizabeth of the Trinity are taken from *I Have Found God: Complete Works of Elizabeth of the Trinity*, vol. 2, *Letters from Carmel*, edited by Conrad De Meester, translated by Anne Englund Nash (Washington, D.C.: ICS Publications, 1995).

The abbreviation for this work is as follows:

L *Letters from Carmel*

St. John of the Cross

All quotations are taken from *The Collected Works of St. John of the Cross*, translated by Kieran Kavanaugh, O.C.D., and Otilio Rodriguez, O.C.D. (Washington, D.C.: ICS Publications, 1991).

The abbreviations for John's works are as follows:

A *The Ascent of Mount Carmel*
C *The Spiritual Canticle*

Co *The Counsels to Religious*

LF *The Living Flame of Love*

For *The Spiritual Canticle*, the first number refers to the stanza and the second number to the paragraph. Thus, C 3.4 is a reference to stanza 3, paragraph 4 of *The Spiritual Canticle*.

St. Teresa of Ávila

All quotations of St. Teresa of Ávila's *Interior Castle* are taken from the Kieran Kavanaugh, O.C.D., and Otilio Rodriguez, O.C.D., translation of *The Collected Works of St. Teresa of Avila*, 3 vols. (Washington, D.C.: ICS Publications, 1976–1985, 1987, 2012).

The abbreviation for this work is as follows:

IC *The Interior Castle*

For *The Interior Castle*, the first number refers to the dwelling place, the second number refers to the chapter, and the third number refers to the paragraph. Thus, IC 3.4.2 refers to the third dwelling place, chapter 4, paragraph 2.

St. Thérèse of Lisieux

All quotations of St. Thérèse of Lisieux are taken from the John Clarke, O.C.D., translation of *Story of a Soul: The Autobiography of St. Thérèse of Lisieux*, 3rd ed. (Washington, D.C.: ICS Publications, 1996).

The abbreviation for this work is as follows:

S *Story of a Soul*

The number following the letter refers to the page of the ICS edition of the work cited. Thus, S 13 refers to page 13 of *Story of a Soul*, third edition, 1996.

Vatican Documents

AA *Apostolicam Actuositatem* (Decree on the Apostolate of the Laity)

AL *Amoris Laetitia* (The Joy of Love)

CCC *Catechism of the Catholic Church*

FC *Familiaris Consortio* (On the Role of the Christian Family in the Modern World)

LG *Lumen Gentium* (Dogmatic Constitution on the Church)

MD *Mulieris Dignitatem* (On the Dignity and Vocation of Women)

INTRODUCTION

CHALLENGES IN MARRIAGE AND FAMILY LIFE THAT HELP US DISCOVER OUR HIDDEN POTENTIAL

When I was working with people with dementia, the consultant psychiatrist said to me, "Contrary to widespread belief that families don't care enough about their elderly relatives, the problem is that they *care so much* that they wear themselves out with trying to look after them." This deeply caring ethos can be generalized to all aspects of family life. But those doing the caring are the last to see themselves as special or heroic, as following a vocation, or as sharing in God's creation; they just get on with the job, doing the best they can.

This book opens the reader to the message of Louis and Zélie Martin: God is present in the everyday struggles of work and family life, and through these struggles, people reach their full potential and become whole and holy. This ordinary couple shows us that those called to married life are embarking on an unknown but amazing journey that will bring them experiences and encounters beyond any expectation.

In preparing to write this book, I tuned my ears to the wavelength of the challenges that married people and families are facing today. They are the people who informed the content, who are the driving force for a book about a nineteenth-century French couple whom the church formally recognized as saints on October 18, 2015.

What are the themes that arise from families of today? It seems parenting has never been more problematic or fraught. Confronted by a bewildering array of baby-care guidelines and child-rearing advice—much of which seems impossible to implement or even directly contradictory—twenty-first-century parents have to negotiate a never-ending series of complex needs and often conflicting priorities. They strive to find a balance that is best for their child, such as feeding regimes and sleep schedules, childcare arrangements and decisions around education and schooling, and employment demands and work schedules. In the longer term they may face fears over job security, the dilemma of furthering one's career or building a business, and the need to provide financially for the family while at the same time establishing a healthy work-life balance, securing "me" time, and also enjoying quality time with the children. All these compete in a world characterized by the relentless demands of social media and the round-the-clock availability it assumes. Single-parent families, those caring for elderly relatives, and families caring for children with sickness, terminal illness, or other special needs face all these problems and more, often with fewer resources and less support.

What on earth can two nineteenth-century parents say to these myriad problems faced by contemporary parents in our frantic and complex world? A surprising amount, it seems, for these challenges and difficulties (albeit in their nineteenth-century forms) are precisely those that Zélie and Louis Martin negotiated in their own marriage and family life. I hope that the following pages will assure today's parents and families that Louis and Zélie are listening to them and understand their troubles, many of which they experienced firsthand in their own lives, and that they are sympathetic, empathic, and above all able to help. As the first married couple to be canonized together, as a union of two people, they are a powerful force!

Louis and Zélie Martin do not give trite or pious answers to these challenges, but they take us on a journey through their experience of marriage and parenthood that has much in common with the issues that concern families today. The chapters guide us through the legacy they brought to their marriage from their own experiences of family life and the effect that had on their relationship. We look at the historical upheaval in which they lived, politically and socially, and the situation of the Catholic Church versus the secular government. Like all young people, they brought their ideals and aspirations to their marriage and needed to make a transition into the reality. We follow the journey of Zélie and Louis through the births and deaths of their children and of their own parents, before looking at the impact of their respective careers on their family life together. Their marriage reaches a climax with the shock of terminal illness, bereavement, and readjustment as a single parent.

Zélie and Louis lived their marriage vows to the hilt, not as pious saints but as ordinary, fallible people who had normal human weaknesses and were subject to fears, joys, and sorrows.

The photographs of family members, stiff and solemn for the camera as they are, reveal them as warm human beings. There are pictures of delightful little girls, a teenager giving the dog a biscuit, daughters beaming from ear to ear because Dad is coming home, and laughter as they sketched each other in the garden. We also see the fine features of the young couple shortly after they married and the sorrow etched on Zélie's face over the death of her children.

Throughout the text, we will hear from Zélie and Louis directly in the words they recorded in diaries and correspondence. I hope to show how they brought to life the sacramentality of marriage, illustrating how Christ can be present in every action. Their unshakable faith in God's presence in the events of each day gives us enormous hope, even amazement. The Martin couple exemplifies how our own struggles and efforts are precious in God's eyes, how beloved we are in his gaze, and how he longs to be present even as we empty the dishwasher, if only we invite him in. If all our actions are rooted in love, every effort made by a mother or father, stepparent or child, and aunt or uncle brings God into the home. "God is love, and those who abide in love abide in God, and God abides in them" (1 Jn 4:16).

There is a temptation to dismiss saints as being of another realm, of another era, or of remote holiness. This disconnection lets us off the hook, so to speak, for an impossible example can have no relevance to our modern lives. As soon as someone is beatified, their halo begins to shine, polished by hands eager to turn them into idealized images of stereotyped sanctity. It is therefore vitally important to stay with the facts and reveal the truth about Louis and Zélie Martin. They and their children were not a perfect family, and they were not perfect parents. France was a secular and anticlerical society that discouraged the integration of Christianity into family life; their local church proclaimed a judgmental God, and the parish life was demanding and heavy on religious rituals. They found their way to holiness, not through visions and ecstasies but through heroism in living family life to the full.

Rather than worrying about how we're already struggling to cope with our full lives without having to fit in any holy practices as well, we can take heart from Louis and Zélie and ask

God to be part of our busy schedules. They give us not a path of perfection but a lifestyle that is simply rooted in love. The daily struggles that cause stress arise because parents care a great deal about providing for their children: their education, their friendships, their health, and their happiness. A yelling match when a teen returns late from a party is the effect of waiting parents' worry and anxiety. Parents worry because they *care*; otherwise no one would be the slightest bit bothered. Because they love, families travel long distances to visit sick sisters or frail grandparents; because they are concerned, they invite lonely neighbors in for Christmas or Thanksgiving; and because they support their children, they join the great care network of grandmas and grandpas that look after their grandchildren so parents can go back to work. Love is present in the family already; through their faith, Louis and Zélie show how God is present and deeply part of that love.

These saint-parents do not give us a parenting manual. They show us that it is more important simply to *be* a parent than to follow a best-seller publication. They found through hard experience that one parenting pattern did not suit every child, but through their struggles and mistakes common to all families, their children developed resilience and determination as adults.

Through their actions, Louis and Zélie demonstrate how children learn from experience. No amount of preaching or teaching will replace taking food to a poor family, learning to cope with insults, fishing with Dad, or shopping with Mom for new outfits. They also show us how much vitality can be gained from doing things together, such as playing hide-and-seek with Dad in the garden, helping Mom with her lace patterns, teaching the pet crow to talk, or making baby brother laugh. Such involvement with their parents' lives adds to the store of memories that become integrated into a developing child's knowledge of the world and repertoire of coping strategies.

So often we are ashamed of our failings, of the apparent cracks in our marriage or family life, but these places are precisely where God is close and our need for him is greater. Louis and Zélie show us how to navigate these cracks in ways that have a sound psychological basis today and, it must be said, how *not* to do things, in the light of modern-day knowledge about attachment theory and bereavement in children. It is reassuring to discover that they were holy because they trusted God and were generous in giving themselves to the task in hand, not because they were always right. God's love was the sap of the vine that flowed through their daily lives and nourished their spirit.

Some fallacies about the Martin family need to be dispelled from the start. Zélie has been described as morbid and obsessed with death. We will see that she was indeed concerned about death, as it was never far away, but in Zélie we will discover a woman of immense energy, vibrant with life. Louis can be portrayed as a lazy man, a "dreamer," who preferred hiding in his prayer room to working and caring for his family, but we will discover a hardworking and fun-loving father who reveled in his children. Perhaps this family was a holy and isolated enclave in the pious French Catholicism of the period, a family where girls were brought up to be nuns and boys (if they survived) to be priests. But we will see a much broader picture. Some point out that these parents had an obsessional and bookkeeping piety that counted sins and demanded payment, all to be added up and reported at the end of each day. This bookkeeping piety was indeed the religious genre of the time, inherited by Zélie and her older sister from their mother. However, being tempered by common sense and humor and the strong experience of being loved, it allowed each member of the family to flourish as adults and discover a God who loved them unconditionally.

Let us look to this couple to see how God became an integral part of family life in a way that the children enjoyed. Children and young people learn about love when they feel they are cherished and belong, when they know they are heard and accepted as they are, for example, when they are praised for trying hard, supported when they are bullied, accepted in their failures or lack of ability in an area, or encouraged as they negotiate friendships.

Teenagers learn to truly value themselves when their attributes such as kindness and generosity are recognized, when they are shown by example how to resolve disputes and quarrels, and when they can recognize and manage conflicting needs and wishes within the family. Young people are truthful; they spot hypocrisy. This Mom and Dad demonstrate an authentic and experiential life of love: love for each other, for the children, for their employees, and for the poor, and underlying all this, absolute certainty that God loved them and that all that happened to them was an expression of his immense love. Little by little, or even by leaps and bounds, their children became deeply grounded and rooted in the practical experience of love.

The questions for reflection at the end of each chapter are there to help us understand and reflect on how these practical experiences of Louis and Zélie can fit into our own circumstances and living of family life. Does their example help us today? What is our own experience, and what did it mean for us at the time, or how is it impacting us now? Have our experiences brought our family closer or driven us apart? In every aspect of our family lives, Louis and Zélie can bring to light the hidden core and root of love, which flourishes into a great tree when it is held in God's love.

I hope that, through this book, Louis and Zélie Martin will emerge as real people who, by sharing their rich and complex lives with couples today, will give them companionship, courage, and a light to guide them on their journey. With St. Paul, they pray "that Christ may dwell in your hearts through faith, as you are being rooted and grounded in love" (Eph 3:17).

1

The Story of a Marriage

God is love, and those who abide in love abide in God, and
God abides in them.

—1 JOHN 4:16

PARENTS FOR TODAY

An Ordinary Couple

A man and a woman enter a registry office in Normandy, France, to be married on Monday, July 12, 1858. Two hours later, at midnight, they bestow on each other the sacrament of marriage in the church of Notre-Dame d'Alençon. Louis Martin is thirty-five and Zélie Guérin is twenty-seven. One hundred and fifty-three years later, on October 18, 2015, Mr. and Mrs. Martin are canonized as a married couple.

This book is about two ordinary people who became saints entirely through their openness to God's grace in the ups and downs of marriage and family life. They offer example and insight not only for married couples but also for those thinking about marriage, those who have been married, and indeed every person, for we all come into existence through the union of a man and a woman, a sperm and an egg.

Holiness through Marriage and Children

The union of Louis and Zélie Martin opens a window into the sacrament of marriage: a view that reveals how every aspect of married life can lead to holiness in parents and in their children. For holiness is not just for the elite; it is another word for *wholeness*, for the full realization of the potential given to every human being when he or she was created "in the image of God" (Gen 1:27). From these parents, now recognized as saints by the Catholic Church, we can learn how God channels this creative love through all ordinary couples who try their best to bring up their family, care for their relatives, earn a living, and provide for their children's future. From Louis and Zélie's rich experience, married people can take heart when sickness overtakes health; parents can be reassured when their child fills them with a sense of helplessness; and sons and daughters can feel supported when their elderly parents need residential care.

Why Get Married?

The question we ask in the freedom of our Western culture today is, why get married? What is marriage? What is the difference between a secular marriage and a Christian marriage, or between a Christian marriage and a wedding within other faiths? All bear witness to a public and legal commitment of two people to each other, a promise mutually given to live together and to care for each other and their children. However, the specific witness given by Louis and Zélie Martin is of their marriage as a *sacrament*, which is an outward sign of inward grace. While the words and actions, the vows and the exchange of rings, take place at the climax of the wedding ceremony, the God-given grace, albeit hidden and invisible at times, flows throughout the marriage.

A wedding is a single event, but a marriage is for life. For this reason, every moment—every relationship, every event—can be sacramental because Christ is present in that union. This is an amazing truth, but St. Paul takes the sacrament even further when he says in his letter to the Ephesians that marriage represents the union of Christ with his church: "'For this reason a man will leave his father and mother and be joined to his wife, and the two will become one flesh.' This is a great mystery, and I am applying it to Christ and the church" (Eph 5:31–32). More vividly, John describes in the book of Revelation his vision of the bride (Jerusalem) of God: "Then one of the seven angels . . . came and said to me, 'Come, I will show you the bride, the wife of the Lamb.' And in the spirit he carried me away to a great, high mountain and showed me the holy city Jerusalem coming down out of heaven from God" (Rev 21:9–10).

This sacrament of marriage is indeed a profound mystery. How can we comprehend it? Theological tomes may explain with didactic reasoning, but they are beyond most of us. Theoretical explanations can dishearten us through their idealistic expectations. The model of the Holy Family living in an occupied country 2,000 years ago seems remote. Perhaps our memory of being parented is too perfect ("I must live up to my father"), so we feel a failure with our own children; or our experiences were painful ("I mustn't do to my children what my parents did to me"), but we are dismayed to find ourselves falling into the same trap. What have a saintly married couple from provincial nineteenth-century France to offer us in the twenty-first century?

Further questions might be raised. Has the Catholic Church made Louis and Zélie Martin saints because they are the holy parents of their well-known and loved youngest child, St. Thérèse of Lisieux? Or perhaps they have been canonized to give us an example of perfect parenthood? Like many saints, will they soon be polished up as too impossibly wonderful to be relevant to us in our own attempts to be good parents? The answer to these concerns lies not in the shine of their halos but in the fact that Louis and Zélie Martin are real people to whom we can relate, a couple who can encourage us by their example in the struggles and even the disasters of our own family lives today.

This particular man and wife were not born as saints; they did not even start their married life as saints. God wrote in their hearts, "You yourselves are our letter, written on our hearts, to be known and read by all; and you show that you are a letter of Christ, prepared by us, written not with ink but with the Spirit of the living God, not on tablets of stone but on tablets of human hearts" (2 Cor 3:2–3).

This couple demonstrates *living* hearts that were not set in a constraining stone of fear but open to the transforming action of the Holy Spirit. They were not hidebound by the Catholic culture of their time but developed *through* their religion and faith. Rather than being overwhelmed by adversity and loss, they were *converted* by their marriage and their children, who were unpredictable in their arrival, their survival, and their needs. If Louis and Zélie had their own ideas of perfection, these were gradually stripped away. With the arrival of children, their calm, well-ordered life was buffeted by heights of joy and depths of despair, as these ordinary parents discovered their own inadequacies and helplessness in the face of adversity. The more they felt a failure, the more they turned to God in blind faith. Their self-competence was transformed to total abandonment to God's love.

We know of many wonderful people we would call saints, but only a few are recognized by the church as models and an inspiration for our times. The Catechism of the Catholic Church tells us,

"The saints have always been the source and origin of renewal in the most difficult moments of the church's history" (*CCC* 192).

SAINTS FOR TODAY

Why Now?

What "difficult moment" are Louis and Zélie Martin addressing in the twenty-first century? Let's look at current trends. From 1970 to 2010, the marriage rate in the United States declined by more than 50 percent. A record low of 51 percent of adults were married in 2010, compared with 72 percent in 1960. The divorce rate is now nearly twice that compared to 1960: up to 50 percent of recent marriages will end in separation prior to the death of a spouse, and 24 percent of children up to the age of twelve will experience divorce.[1]

Of the 50 percent of adults in the United States who choose to have a wedding, many opt for a civil ceremony, perhaps with personalized marriage vows in a beautiful setting for the "perfect day." In the ensuing months and years challenges inevitably emerge, and the couple, thrown on their own resources, may struggle to stay together. The concept of ongoing sacramental *grace* that enables two people to commit themselves to love and to cherish each other until death do them part is foreign to them. Sadly, they are also oblivious to the other face of this rich coin of grace: *God's* commitment to the married couple. In a sacramental marriage, God's contract with these two mutually chosen people gives them cause to hope and trust in God,

---

1. See the website for "Key Statistics from the National Survey of Family Growth," Centers for Disease Control and Prevention, last updated October 13, 2017, accessed February 27, 2017, *https://www.cdc.gov/*.

to worry less about their ability to make the marriage "work." God has it all in hand.

Zélie Speaks

As she was a great letter writer, we will let Zélie speak for herself.[2] Sharing her worries and vivid observations with her brother, Isidore, her sister-in-law, Céline, or her daughter, Pauline (at boarding school), the following excerpts would not be out of place in an "advice column" today.

> I have a violent headache and I'm up against constant aggravation. Moreover, we have my father-in-law who is near death; I don't think he'll live another two weeks. He's dying of old age; already half his body is paralyzed. (CF 13)

> I confess, death terrifies me. (CF 14)

> My childhood, my youth was as sad as a shroud because, if my mother spoiled [my brother], she was too strict with me. (CF 15)

> [My business] is going badly, completely badly, it couldn't go any worse. I positively believe I am at the end of my reign. (CF 32)

> I don't know which way to turn any more. I'm up from four-thirty in the morning until eleven o'clock at night. All my time should be for my father [who was dying], and I shouldn't have anything else on my mind. (CF 33)

---

2. All quotes are taken from Zélie and Louis Martin, *A Call to a Deeper Love: The Family Correspondence of the Parents of Saint Thérèse of the Child Jesus, 1863–1885*, ed. Frances Renda, trans. Ann Connors Hess (New York: Society of St. Paul, 2011). The letters will be referred to as "CF" (*Correspondance Familiale*) in the text.

I'm even more inclined to constantly blame myself for my little Hélène's death [she died aged five years], but I never thought for a moment it would end like that. (CF 53)

Oh well, I'm truly not very pleasant. Fortunately, I'm still willing to admit it! But if I don't know how to show signs of affection, I feel the sentiments inside. (CF 138)

But I have too many worries to have total peace of mind, problems with clothes that never end! . . . You can say again, we're never satisfied! . . . all of that [shopping for clothes] is a veritable slavery, and one is truly a slave to fashion! (CF 143, 151)

Zélie poured out her hopes and fears through her pen, but her rock of strength was her husband. Louis, in contrast to his vivacious and work-driven wife, was quiet, contemplative, and solitary. As the saying goes, "opposites attract," and indeed they complemented each other. Perhaps Zélie was drawn to Louis because he brought her the unconditional gentleness, love, and support that she never experienced in her own childhood, and she in her turn brought him the energy, zest for life, and social ease that he found difficult to express. This mutually enhancing partnership provided a resilient foundation for the family that was to come. As pieces of a puzzle interlock uniquely to make one picture, their many facets found a home in each other to create a warm hearth for children, work, employees, relatives, and friends.

Honed by Circumstances

However, no relationship remains static. As we follow the deep river of Louis and Zélie's marriage and parenting experience, we will see that their sanctity was honed by the mistakes and struggles as well as the joys and achievements that families experience today.

The iron strength of their Christian marriage was forged in a social furnace of national secularism—how modern is that? Louis and Zélie allowed the grace of marriage to work through them to give witness to Christ in an environment of political turmoil, a nation humiliated by war and loss of empire, and a country ravaged by floods and financial collapse. It was a tumultuous period of industrial change and spread of infection in a pre-antibiotic age.

The story of these people in nineteenth-century Normandy might appear distant to us in time and in culture, but it unfolded only fifty years or so before the Allied invasion of Normandy on Tuesday, June 6, 1944, which contributed to the end of the Second World War.

We may ourselves have cherished records of grandparents and great-grandparents from that time of world conflict. We can also open the pages of the Martin family album, thanks to the many photographs taken by Céline (the second-youngest Martin daughter). The black-and-white portraits of men, women, and children stiffly keeping still for the camera could be of grandpa or grandma, great-aunt, or great-uncle in our own family albums. They look like our family, they are ordinary people like us, and they show us how we too can allow our everyday family lives to be places of transforming grace.

Discovery and Growth

Indeed, the everyday life of this couple involved a hardworking mom, financial insecurity, grief and bereavement, separation and loss, boarding school and being bullied, childhood illness, mental health problems, single fatherhood, and other issues we see today as well. How did they survive? In her book *The Interior Castle*, St. Teresa of Ávila says,

> We cannot know whether or not we love God, although there are strong indications for recognizing that we do love Him; but we can know whether we love our neighbor. I believe that, since our nature is bad, we will not reach perfection in the love of neighbor if that love doesn't arise from love of God as its root. (IC 5.3.8–9)

We will see how Louis and Zélie's marriage and all its difficulties brought them to trust and love one another ever more deeply. Their severe trials did not dismay and depress but were the gateway into a positive cycle in which their trust in God was expressed as love for the family, and this love for each other in its turn deepened their reliance on God. The challenging events and relationships within family life enhanced and revealed the hidden depths within each family member.

What are these hidden depths? Describing the soul as a castle made entirely out of a diamond or of very clear crystal, Teresa of Ávila tells us: "I don't find anything comparable to the magnificent beauty of a soul and its marvelous capacity. Indeed, our intellects, however keen, can hardly comprehend it" (IC 1.1.1). Most of us are only dimly aware (if at all) of this lovely place deep within us where God chooses to dwell, distracted as we are by the busyness of daily life. But the strains and joys of living in a family can open a window into our inmost hearts, revealing our hidden potential and capacity to love.

It is unlikely we will always *feel* love, but commitment to another person changes us. As life together unfolds, I find that my spouse and (especially) our children hold up a mirror to me, showing my true self. Pushed to the limit of my energy levels, my tolerance, my anxieties, my abilities, I discover an inner self that I didn't know existed, a self that can give and receive unconditional love. At different stages of family life, I find myself letting go of old ways of doing things and am freed up for new ways, new growth toward wholeness, holiness.

In the next chapters, we will let Louis and Zélie Martin show us how their growth together is relevant for us today, how they offer us a practical married spirituality, and most of all, how God is present in all the little and daily events of our family life, however desperate that life is at times.

QUESTIONS FOR REFLECTION

- How has your experience of marriage, whether your own marriage, your parents' marriage, your engagement to be married, or seeing others get married, changed you? Has this experience deepened your trust in God, or has it made him seem more distant?

- How do you see the sacramentality of marriage? Can you think of any small actions or events this week that have reflected this sacrament of God's presence?

- Do you believe that God loves you unconditionally, just as you are? How does he reveal that love through the events and relationships of your family life?

2

A Man and a Woman of Their Past

Before I formed you in the womb I knew you,
and before you were born I consecrated you.

—JEREMIAH 1:5

GREAT EXPECTATIONS

Each one of us is known by God our Father before we are conceived. The time and place in which we start our lives provide the melting pot in which we are formed: genes and environment interact to offer a rich brew in which we can grow and flourish. Gently, through discovery of our talents and deepest desires, and through our achievements and apparent failures, God guides us to the purpose for which he created us. As he prepared Jeremiah to be a prophet, God prepares each one of us for our own unique roles, through our families, our childhood, our cultural heritage, and the historical events in which we live.

A Child Is Born

The child is not born into a vacuum. Parents, grandparents, and even the wider family will have expectations regarding the

19

expected baby or adopted child. Thoughts, spoken or unspoken, express the hopes and fears that brood in every family and prepare the ground for the newcomer. These may be aspirations such as, "he will continue the family line"; "she will be the girl we have all been longing for"; "she will replace my daughter who died"; "he will follow in his father's footsteps"; "she will be a sister for her disabled brother"; or "he will be a priest." In looking at how God transformed Louis and Zélie through their families and experiences, we can be confident that God is holding us safe within our own experiences, however discomforting they may be.

Sometimes it is difficult to find individual identity in the forest of family expectations. Children initially discover who they are through the way their own selves are reflected to them. Watch a small baby interacting with its mom or dad; see the reflection in the parent's eyes, the smile on their faces, and the singing in their voices as they respond to the baby's gurgles and cries. Infants see delight on their parents' faces, so they feel delightful; they absorb warmth from their parents and feel treasured. Sadly, the opposite is also true, and children who only see condemnation and disapproval in the eyes of their caregivers feel inadequate and useless.

Two Childhoods Brought Together

Zélie experienced a childhood that made her ache with sadness, as we shall see. She arrived at marriage with skills born of growing up in an atmosphere of chill duty and, after leaving home, of negotiating apparent failure to forge a new path as an independent young woman. She was reliant on the motherly support of her older sister, known as Élise, and in turn cared for her much younger brother, Isidore, as a mother.

Resigned to suffering, Zélie expected little from others but took it upon herself to carry responsibility for others' security and happiness. Opening her heart to the needs of those around her, she made huge demands on herself through hard work, loyalty to her family, caring for those in need, and above all, making her Catholic faith the pivot of each demanding day. With a legacy of frailty as a child who was prone to illness and recurrent migraines, she would feel overwhelmed at times, sick, exhausted, and anxious. Louis, in a letter written from Paris, would later admonish her, "Needless to say, your letter made me very happy, except I see that you've tired yourself out *far too much*. So I *strongly* recommend calm and moderation, above all, in your work . . . once again, don't worry *so much*" (CF 2-a; emphasis added). For a quietly spoken man who chose his words carefully, Louis here used strong language!

What did Louis bring to the marriage? As will be seen, his youthful plans came to nothing. He was not inclined to follow his family's military tradition, was rejected as a monk, and then failed in his attempts to master Latin. Did he bring a sense of failure into his marriage? It seems that, far from being bowed down, he rose to the challenge of changing his perspective and focusing on a career as a watchmaker. His response to his unfulfilled yearning to religious life was that if he couldn't be a monk in a monastery, he would be a monk in the world. He would remain single, follow his chosen profession, and live simply and in solitude, finding enough social outlets through the church, good works, and religious meetings. However, how could this vision of personal holiness accord with married life?

These are the real difficulties Louis and Zélie brought to their marriage. Their premarital adaptations to life's slings and arrows would have to be worked out together, resolved and healed through God's grace working through this powerful sacrament. Their mutual bestowal of marriage would gradually release them from their earlier but now redundant coping methods, making them free to become shining lights to reveal the effects of grace on our humanity.

GREAT FAMILY TRADITIONS

The Heritage Carried by Zélie

What were the family influences that formed Zélie Guérin? Courage, in the face of both religious persecution and military life, stands out. Her great-uncle Guillaume was ordained a priest in 1786, just three years before the storming of the Bastille, which launched the French Revolution. Courageously refusing compulsory "constitutional service" (military service) in 1791, he continued to minister as a priest underground, celebrating clandestine Masses and seeing churches desecrated and monks and nuns evicted from their monasteries. He survived seven years in this hidden ministry before being denounced by a fellow priest and imprisoned at Alençon's jail. After nine months in his prison cell, he was deported to Ile de Ré, a small, flat island off the west coast of France, from where he was released after two years and could return to his pastoral role as a curate. This brave and priestly Uncle Guillaume was part of the Guérin family's strong Catholic tradition, a family whose members "liked to tell the adventures of their great-uncle Guillaume who was a priest during the French Revolution."[1] We can understand how his example could have reinforced Zélie's tendency to see

---

1. Hélène Mongin, *The Extraordinary Parents of St. Thérèse of Lisieux*, trans. Marsha Daigle-Williamson (Huntington, Ind.: Our Sunday Visitor, 2015), 16.

suffering in the face of adversity as heroic and a necessary path to salvation.

Zélie's father, Isidore Guérin, grew up in a post-revolution climate of persecution and antireligious violence that he often evoked through his memories and stories when he was spending his last days with Zélie and Louis and their family. As a young man, in 1807, he bucked the family tradition of agriculture in favor of a more exciting life as a soldier on Napoleon Bonaparte's battlefields, fighting in Germany, Portugal, and Spain. Much later, in 1857, he would be awarded the St. Helena medal, instigated by Napoleon III from his island of exile of that name, in recognition of military service during the 1792–1815 Napoleonic campaigns.[2]

Following an injury in Spain, this brave officer was obliged to leave the army life he loved in 1813, but he transferred his experience and skills to the French foot police, later the mounted police. A handsome man of thirty-nine, he doubtless cut a dashing figure in his uniform, and in 1828, he won the heart of Louise-Jeanne Macé, aged twenty-three, the only daughter of a close military friend. They had two daughters, Élise and Zélie and, ten years later, a son, Isidore. Isidore Sr. retired from the police force in 1844 and bought a house in Alençon, where he would remain the rest of his life.

Zélie was to take her father under her wing after her mother died in 1859, revealing a deep tenderness for this gruff old soldier who delighted in his grandchildren but did not have the words to show affection for her as a child.

---

2. The St. Helena medal was awarded to approximately 305,000 Frenchmen and 55,000 foreigners. For more information, see "Order of Saint Louis," Wikipedia, last updated January 23, 2018, *https://en.wikipedia.org/wiki/Order_of_Saint_Louis/*.

After their father's retirement, the teenage girls (Élise was fifteen and Zélie thirteen) benefited from a good education at the school of the Religious of the Sacred Hearts of Jesus and Mary in Alençon, of which Élise said later, "To be able to pray and to study at ease was like paradise."[3] Zélie excelled at composition and writing, winning the prize for literary style, as she said in a letter to her brother: "The more I say to you, the more you'll tease me about my style; I'm certain of it. . . . I did, however, win first prize in style in the past. Out of eleven compositions, I won first prize ten times, and then I was in the first division and in the upper class. So judge the ability of the others!" (CF 3).

School offered respite, but home life was stressful for the girls. The hand of their severely religious mother, whose own father died when she was only five, dealt out discipline and austerity, particularly toward her middle child, Zélie. With her much younger brother, Isidore, protected as the baby and the only boy, and her sister, Élise, privileged as the eldest child, this sensitive middle child was constantly ill and suffered recurrent migraines. Soon after her marriage to Louis, and desperately sad that her little brother had decided to move from Alençon to Lisieux, she reminded him of her childhood years: "But what you want makes it necessary to give up everything. I never had much joy in my life, no, never what one would call joy. My childhood, my youth, was as sad as a shroud because, if my mother spoiled you, as you know, she was too strict with me. She, though so good, didn't know how to treat me, so my heart suffered greatly" (CF 15). This word *shroud*, the funeral sheet used

---

3. Jean Clapier, *Louis et Zélie Martin: Une sainteté pour tous les temps* (Paris: Presses de la Renaissance, un département d'Édi8, 2009), 51. (Unless otherwise noted, all translations are my own.)

to cover a dead person, gives us an indication of how dead this little girl felt inside.

After his retirement, Zélie's father enlarged the house in Alençon for his young family and then revamped it as a café with a billiard room on the first floor, hoping thereby to make a bit of money. Unfortunately, the severe Madame Guérin put customers off with her moralizing, and the café soon had to close. Money was tight so Élise and Zélie were made busy doing their share of hard work during the school holidays.

From this severe and sad start to her life, Zélie emerged as a young woman of determination and courage but with an anxious nature and a need to be useful and get things right. A good student, she completed her secondary education and then sought to work with the sick and the poor in Alençon by joining the religious order of the Daughters of Charity. Her mother, who disapproved of Zélie's mission, came with her to meet the superior, who conclusively told Zélie that she did not have a vocation to be a nun! Zélie, like Louis, was deeply disappointed but took the rejection as a fait accompli and changed direction to study for two years (1851–1853) at the famous Alençon school of lacemaking. She had a natural talent for the intricate beauty of the work, and after hands-on work as an employee in the industry, she set up a successful business with the help of Élise and their mother. Now an independent young woman only twenty-two, in bourgeois French culture she was still considered young for marriage.

Zélie arrived on the lace scene at the right time, for the Alençon factory had fallen with the French Empire, and by 1830 there were only two or three hundred laceworkers employed. Ten years later, some older women with experience in making the fine lace were brought back to pass on their skill, and a few samples of lace were shown at the 1851 Great Exhibition at Crystal Palace in London. The turnaround happened in 1856, when large orders were placed for the layette of the prince imperial, the infant Napoleon. The coverlet of his little bed was to be of Alençon lace. In addition, the christening robe, mantle, and headdress; twelve dozen embroidered frocks; and the nurses' aprons were all to be trimmed with the now fashionable *point d'Alençon!* In 1859, the costliest work ever executed at Alençon was exhibited. This was a dress valued at 200,000 francs, which was purchased by the Emperor Napoleon III for the empress.

Five years on, Élise, who was not to be deterred after facing many setbacks, entered the Visitation convent in Le Mans (about thirty miles from Alençon), saying, "I come here to be a saint." Zélie was devastated, having never been separated from her elder sister, closest friend and now business partner, a sister whose future as a religious was assured. Where was her own life to take her?

Another strong woman, who had met Zélie on a lace-making course, stepped into the scene. She was Fanie Martin (née Fanie Boureau), a mother who was determined to steer her sole remaining child, Louis, away from life as a bachelor. Impressed by Zélie's spirituality, determination, and talent, she set about persuading her son to consider marriage. The Holy Spirit moved quickly, and in just three months, Zélie and Louis were married! But how could Zélie find holiness in marriage? She still yearned for religious life and wept on her wedding day.

The Heritage Carried by Louis

The middle child of three sisters and a brother, Louis was the survivor in his family. He was about fifteen when his elder brother drowned, nineteen when his nine-year-old sister died, and twenty when his brother-in-law died eight months after Louis's sister. His second sister passed away when he was twenty-two, and his remaining sister died when he was thirty. Only Adolph, his nephew, remained, to whom Louis later sold his business. Like Zélie, Louis grew up in a military household with a tradition of bravery and honor. His maternal great-uncle, François Bohard, was the family hero; during the French Revolution, he saved the bells of his parish church from the revolutionary guards by hiding them under his clothing. Louis's father, Pierre-François, had a wonderful combination of religious depth and military fervor. He campaigned with Napoleon Bonaparte's army in Prussia and Poland, then with the Royalist army.

In 1818, Pierre-François was visiting a military colleague and close friend when he met and fell in love with his daughter, Fanie Boureau. He was forty-one, and she was just eighteen when they married in 1818. Six years later Pierre-François was decommissioned and made a knight of the Royal and Military Order of St. Louis in recognition of his long military service as an officer.[4] His second son, Louis, was just one year old. After he fulfilled civic responsibilities in Avignon and Strasbourg, the family settled in Alençon in 1830, when Louis was seven and his father had finally retired from army life.

Louis did not attend high school, but the good education provided for the son of an officer up to the age of fourteen or fifteen bore fruit in his love of literature and motivation to learn a profession. He could have followed in his father's footsteps, but since Napoleon's defeat, the French army was oversubscribed

---

4. The Royal and Military Order of St. Louis was founded by Louis XIV in 1693 and reinstated by Louis XVIII. Abolished in 1830, it is a predecessor of the Legion of Honor, with whom it shares the red ribbon.

and had lost its allure. Moreover, Louis felt more drawn to solitude and reflection than to adventure in battle.

During a stay with his uncle, a watchmaker in Rennes, Louis discovered his hidden talent: he would take up the same profession. To this end, he completed the basic training in Rennes, where he discovered and relished the writings of well-known French authors such as Chateaubriand, Bossuet, and Fénelon. His literary taste revealed his sensitive nature and his deep awareness of beauty, whether in literature or in the Brittany countryside. His long walks were a prayer of marveling at the beauty of creation.

On one of his long rambles in Switzerland, Louis came across the Great St. Bernard hospice, founded in the eleventh century to care for Alpine travelers. Straddling the Great St. Bernard Pass 8,000 feet above sea level, this hostelry still offers a haven for mountaineers. It offered an attractive life for a fit young man who wanted to care for others, live in a community, and follow an ordered routine of prayer and service in such a stunning environment. The icy cold winds and austere way of life would have been no deterrent to this son of a military man. On the contrary, it offered him a challenge to explore, not the world in battle, but the inner world in tranquility.

Louis was now twenty-two years old and not inclined to make any hasty decisions. He gave time for this possible vocation to mature while he pursued further watchmaking studies at Strasbourg for two years. Here this serious young man enjoyed the balance of life between prayer, his studies, and religious meetings with his friends that would often end with a game of billiards.

As was Zélie in her quest for religious life, Louis was deeply disappointed when he finally knocked on the door of the Great

St. Bernard monastery only to be told that, as he had no Latin skills, he must complete his secondary education before reapplying. He tried very hard to fulfill this requirement, even employing a tutor for 120 Latin lessons, but the stress of the difficult studies made him so ill that he took it as a sign pointing him away from monastic life.

Louis returned to his other calling and undertook an apprenticeship in Paris to become a master clock and watch maker. This was a period of political turmoil leading up to the French Revolution of 1848, when the archbishop of Paris would be shot dead. It was a time of temptation for a handsome young man, for the yoke of religious morals had been cast aside by the revolutionary spirit, but also a time of risk, for sexual freedom meant that diseases such as syphilis were rife. Later he was to warn his young brother-in-law against the perils of Paris, through a letter from Zélie: "Every day my husband makes sad predictions. He knows Paris, and he tells me that you'll be up against temptations that you'll find hard to resist because you're not religious enough. He told me what temptations he had and the courage he needed to overcome his struggles. If you only knew what ordeals he went through. . . . I beg you, my dear Isidore, do as he did; *pray*, and you will not let yourself be carried away by the torrent. If you give in once, you're lost" (CF 1).

Louis was twenty-seven when he moved back to the tranquility of Alençon in 1845 to set up shop. Here he could live a quasi-monastic life of work, silence, and prayer, not forgetting his rambles in the countryside and fishing on Sundays (He was nicknamed by his friends "Fisherman Martin"). He had no desire to be married and indeed, in 1857, bought the "Pavilion," a small octagonal tower near his house, where he could escape the world to read and pray in solitude. He turned down a proposed match

with a suitable young woman, saying that her family was too lib-
eral, but in reality, his ideal was to live a celibate life.

However, his mother was that wise woman, Fanie, whose
hopes for her remaining daughter, Fany, were dashed when she
died in 1853. Having told Louis about a fine young woman she
had met on a lace-making course who had the same spiritual
depth as himself, Fanie was determined to arrange an early meeting for the young couple. However, her plans were preempted
by the Holy Spirit, for Zélie came across Louis by chance on St.
Leonard Bridge in Alençon and heard an inner voice of inspiration that this tall, dignified, and noble-looking man walking
toward her was the one God had prepared for her to marry. They
spoke to each other on the bridge and found they could share so
much that they did indeed fall for each other. Their courtship
was short and formal as was the custom at the time, and the lack
of a dowry for Zélie was not a problem for the Martin family.
The two exchanged vows on July 13, 1858.

SELF-DISCOVERY IN MARRIAGE

We have seen that Louis and Zélie shared much in common
from their family backgrounds, but what would Zélie, with her
sad memories of childhood, bring to this marriage? She certainly brought determination, resilience, and self-sufficiency.
As a woman setting up her own lace business, she was an
entrepreneur. Not one to enjoy any frivolous entertainments,
she had a strong work ethic and mistrusted a search for happiness as the world saw it, asking only that God would fulfill his
will for her in marriage. Family was important to her, and her
letters open windows for us to share in her heartfelt relationships with her sister, brother, and father. Having grown up in a

penny-pinching household, she was determined to ensure that her own children would each have the dowry she never had to start them off in life, and even more, she wanted to give them the happy home she had never had. Zélie had a clear vision of her vocation to marriage.

Always busy and a bit of a worrier, Zélie married a man who brought her balance. As a person who was contemplative by nature, Louis answered her hidden longing. He fulfilled her need for security and a safe haven while giving her the freedom to run her business and manage her household. As a father who loved to play and sing with their children, take them to the countryside, tell them stories, and teach them about heroic saints, he combined forces with her to provide a happy home.

The lonely girl, "as miserable as a shroud," could blossom into a strong and fulfilled woman. Always a "Martha," "distracted by many things," she married a "Mary," "who sat at the Lord's feet and listened to what he was saying" (Lk 10:38–42), and the two became one in the sacrament of marriage. She launched on a journey of discovery. Her heart sang the same tune as another bride; as Isaiah sings of Jerusalem, Zélie was delightful:

> You shall be a crown of beauty in the hand of the Lord,
> and a royal diadem in the hand of your God.
> You shall no more be termed Forsaken,
> and your land shall no more be termed Desolate;
> but you shall be called My Delight Is in Her,
> and your land Married;
> for the Lord delights in you,
> and your land shall be married. (Isa 62:3–4)

Louis found a wife who balanced his propensity to be a recluse, who drew him out from himself. Her mind on his wavelength, he could talk to her freely about the things that mattered deeply to him: things of God, of creation, of beauty. Zélie was also a great friend and companion, filling the void formed by the loss of his brothers and sisters. He could share with her his love of the church and the many religious confraternities and associations in which they participated. He would bring high ideals to the marriage, perhaps too high, for he was still a monk at heart and believed the purest form of marriage was one of celibacy.

Here we have two people shaped by their early life experiences, for whom marriage provided the hallowed space to completely fulfill God's will through the heights and depths of family life. But first, how was their marriage shaped by the dramatic social, political, and religious events of their time?

QUESTIONS FOR REFLECTION

- Did you feel treasured and "delightful" as a child? What impact does that early experience, or lack of it, have on your relationship with those at home? What difference does it make that God delights in you and everything you do for your family?

- Do you expect those close to you to fulfill your needs, or do you relish their differences and foibles? Would you like to change any aspects of yourself?

- What hopes and expectations from your family are you carrying on your shoulders? Are they inspiring, or do they make you feel a failure? What are God's desires for you?

3

A Time of Upheaval

Political events	Year(s)	Family and church events
American Revolution	1765	
	1777	*Louis's father born*
American War of Independence	1775–1783	
	1786	*Zélie's great-uncle Guillaume Guérin ordained*
French Revolution, Storming of the Bastille	1789	30,000 priests exiled, hundreds more killed *Zélie's father born*
First Republic	1792–1804	Pope Pius VI exiled by French troops
	1798	*Great-uncle Guillaume imprisoned and exiled*
	1799–1824	*Louis's father's military career*
First Empire: Napoleon Bonaparte I	1804–1830	
	1806	*Zélie's mother born*

Continued

Political events	Year(s)	Family and church events
	1807–1813	*Zélie's father's military career*
French Restoration (Louis XVIII & Charles X)	1814–1830	
Battle of Waterloo	1815	
	1823	*Louis born*
July Revolution	1830	Apparition of Our Lady of the Miraculous Medal
July Monarchy (Louis-Philippe)	1830–1848	
	1831	*Zélie born*
	1832	Locution of Our Lady of Victories
	1846	Apparition of Our Lady of La Salette
Revolution of 1848	1848	Archbishop of Paris shot dead
Second Republic	1848–1852	
	1850	*Louis leaves Paris for Alençon*
Second Empire: Napoleon III	1852–1870	
	1853	The railway arrives at Alençon
	1854	Doctrine of Our Lady of the Immaculate Conception
	1858	February 11–July 16: 18 apparitions of our Lady at Lourdes

Continued

Political events	Year(s)	Family and church events
	1858	July 13: *Louis and Zélie married*
Third Republic	1870–1940	
Franco-Prussian War	1870–1871	
	1871	January 15–March 7: Prussian occupation of Alençon
		January 17: Apparition of Our Lady of Pontmain
Paris Commune crushed	1871	Archbishop of Paris and 64 clerics shot dead
	1873	*Thérèse born*
	1877	*Zélie dies*
Jules Ferry (Minister of Public Instruction) legislation	1879–1885	Secularization of state schools
	1883	*Louis's mother dies*
	1894	*Louis dies*
	1897	*Thérèse dies*
Persecution of the Catholic Church	1901–1905	30,000 to 60,000 priests and nuns exiled
Law of Separation of the Churches and the State	1905	Catholic schools and universities closed

We have looked at the gifts and expectations Louis and Zélie brought to their marriage from their earlier experiences and their family histories, but how was the world into which their marriage was born going to influence them? Were the dramatic events of nineteenth-century France to have much impact on their day-to-day lives?

The very complexity of France's history that is entwined in the life stories of Louis and Zélie Martin and their families adds grist to the mill of their sanctity. Our own lives today are affected by national and world events: acts and threats of terrorism, migration, diseases such as the Ebola virus and COVID-19, and natural disasters such as drought, wildfires, and floods. Our history is made by our ancestors, perhaps our own grandparents or great-grandparents; the wars and conflicts, laws and social policies, and economic and financial strategies of previous generations all shape the world in which we live today. Louis and Zélie, far from being disconnected from worldly realities, allowed the history they inherited and the events through which they lived to hone and deepen their trust in God, their relationship with each other, and their determination to protect their children.

EMPIRES AND REPUBLICS

It would take another book to chronicle all the complexities of France's tortuous history in this period, but it is helpful to place it in the context of the Martin and Guérin family histories. Using the timeline at the start of this chapter as a template, we can follow the sequence of key social and political changes in parallel with their family events in rural Normandy. Strangely enough, the story starts with the American War of Independence (1775–1783). France supported the Americans with money, arms, and soldiers, and by 1779 the French debt incurred to fight in that war came to 1.3 billion *livres* (about thirteen billion dollars today). Six years on, the experience of fighting in a revolution against the establishment of English royalty and landowners, and starvation in the streets, combined to spark the start of the French Revolution with the Storming of the Bastille in 1789. The same year marked the birth of the First French Republic and the birth of Zélie's father, a year when thousands of priests and religious were exiled or killed, and French troops expelled Pope Pius VI (who had condemned the revolution) from the Papal States. This was when Zélie's great-uncle Guillaume was imprisoned and exiled by the republican guards for refusing to give up his ministry as a Catholic priest.

First Empire

The First French Republic brought the rise of a young man short in stature but tall in military strategy, Napoleon Bonaparte I. A star in the Republic, he was emperor from 1804 to 1814 and initially won every battle due to brilliant tactics throughout his expansion of the French Empire in Europe. Louis's father, Pierre-François, enjoyed a distinguished military career fighting in Napoleon's campaigns, as did Zélie's father over a briefer period. However, success engenders enemies, and overstretching his army in his ambition to take Moscow, Napoleon was finally defeated. He abdicated in 1814, when the monarchy was restored. Sixteen years on, the July Revolution of 1830 inaugurated the "July Monarchy." Zélie was born in 1831.

Second Republic

The July Monarchy of Louis-Philippe terminated with a second French revolution in 1848, when the archbishop of Paris was shot dead. These events had a deep impact on Louis, who was in the capital from 1847 to 1849 to complete his apprenticeship as a watchmaker. During the ensuing Second Republic, Louis bought his shop premises in Alençon, and Zélie was rejected by the Daughters of Charity.

Second Empire

France became an empire again in 1852 under Napoleon III, the nephew of Napoleon I. Famous for the rebuilding of Paris, Napoleon III financed the industrial revolution, modernized farming methods to prevent seasons of famine, and encouraged commercial innovations such as building the first departmental store in Paris. (On a European pilgrimage with her father, Thérèse of Lisieux was amazed by the elevators, likening their capacity to speed one upward to the efficacy of prayer). Napoleon's expansion of roads and railways not only enabled workers to flock to the factories but also linked up the regions of France to make a unified nation.

Third Republic

Like his famous uncle, Napoleon was overambitious to expand the Second Empire and engaged in one disastrous battle after another. He finally suffered a humiliating defeat on September 1, 1870, at the Battle of Sedan, during the Franco-Prussian War, and was exiled to the island of St. Helena (from where he awarded the St. Helena campaign medal to Zélie's father). The Third Republic was hastily formed to bring order out of chaos that, despite ongoing tension between the royalists (mainly Catholics and military) and the republicans, would persist until the start of the Second World War in 1940.

After the Battle of Sedan, the Prussian army invaded France and laid siege to Paris for four months before signing the Franco-Prussian Armistice on January 28, 1871. This agreement left France penniless after paying a huge ransom and resulted in the collapse of the stock market.

The Paris Commune

Discontent in the unemployed workers and resistance to the new government led to barricades being built once again on the streets of Paris by the "Paris Commune," reminiscent of the first French revolution in 1789. The unrest culminated in the Bloody Week of May 21–28, 1871, when at least ten thousand of these "communards" were killed by the regular army of the Republic. Before being slaughtered themselves, the communards shot the archbishop of Paris and sixty-four priests whom they had held to ransom. Six years before her own death in 1877, Zélie represented many French people when she said, "Everything that's happening in Paris fills my soul with sadness. I just learned of the death of the Archbishop and sixty-four priests who were shot yesterday by the Communards. I'm very, very distressed by it" (CF 66).

CHURCH AND STATE

Anticlericalism

Secularism, anticlericalism, and anti-Semitism were in the warp and weave of French bourgeois life during the Second Republic, just as they are issues for us now. *La Lanterne* was a daily political journal with the cover-page message "Voila l'ennemi!" (This is the enemy!). It enticed its readers with lurid front covers such as a snarling red devil depicting clericalism and the church, or an obese friar guzzling food and wine in his spacious cell while a lady of the night entices him with her smile through the window.

The anticlericalism faction wanted to remove the power and authority of the church. To restrict the influence of the church over the education system, legislation enacted by Jules Ferry between 1879 and 1885 would reform the state schools and drastically restrict the number of religious orders authorized to run "outdated" Catholic schools. Orders banned from teaching would include the Visitation Order (of which Zélie's sister was a member) and the Benedictine Order, both of which educated the Martin children.

The anticlericalism of post-revolution France promoted secularism that was to lead to intense persecution of the Catholic Church from 1901, only four years after Thérèse, the Martin's youngest daughter, died. Initially, eighty-one congregations of women and fifty-four of men were dissolved, but in 1904, almost all the religious orders were banned and between 30,000 and 60,000 priests, nuns and religious brothers were exiled. Separation of church and state was made law in 1905, when any surviving Catholic schools and educational establishments were closed.

Apparitions of Our Lady—Why Now?

It is difficult to imagine the impact of this virulent anticlericalism on the average French Catholic. The churches remained empty. The largely Catholic population was no longer in the habit of attending Mass or of contributing to the social matrix of parish life. The Catholic Church was stripped of her powers and her role in society. More than this, all references to Christianity were suspect; even the annual calendar, hinged as it is on the birth of Christ, came under threat of returning to that dated from the French Revolution, the Republican Calendar promulgated in 1793.

Into this spiritual vacuum an extraordinary intervention took place: Mary the Mother of God made herself seen and heard. She first appeared the year before Zélie was born, to a young novice with the Daughters of Charity, Catherine Labouré, just a week before the July Revolution of 1830 that put Louis-Philippe on the throne. Over several apparitions, she foretold the tribulations that were to come and asked Catherine to have a medal made of herself as the the Immaculate Conception, now known popularly around the world as "the Miraculous Medal."

Two years later, Our Lady of Victories spoke to a humble parish priest in his empty church of that name in Paris (built by King Louis XIII in thanksgiving for his victories), asking him to set up an Association of the Immaculate Heart of Mary. This Father Charles, who was about to resign in despair because so few came to Mass or the sacraments despite his best efforts, told his sparse Sunday congregation that there would be a first meeting of the association after Vespers that evening. He returned without much hope a few hours later, only to find his church full!

Our Lady then appeared to two children, Mélanie Calvat and Maximin Giraud in La Salette in 1846, as they returned home with the family's few cows, not long before the revolution of 1848 when the archbishop of Paris was shot dead. Speaking in their own dialect, she gave a message of hope and reconciliation for all humanity.

Our Lady of Lourdes is known throughout the world. She appeared eighteen times to young Bernadette Soubirous in 1858, when they prayed the rosary together and the healing waters of Lourdes pushed out from the dry earth. Healing waters would also flow from another memorable event during that blessed year: the meeting of Louis and Zélie on the bridge in Alençon.

The final apparition of Mary during Louis and Zélie's lifetime was that of Our Lady of Pontmain, who appeared to Joseph and Eugene Barbadette on January 17, 1871, at the height of the Prussian invasion. That same day the Prussian forces withdrew, and the long-awaited armistice ending the Franco-Prussian War was signed one week later.

Our Lady's interventions had an exponential impact on the depleted and disheartened Catholic population. Following the Blessed Mother's appearance to young Catherine Labouré, the Miraculous Medal rapidly sold in its millions due to its healing impact on people's lives, and Pope Pius IX proclaimed the Doctrine of the Immaculate Conception four years later. The medal's profound symbolism of Mary's love and care for those caught up in the disasters of their time still brings hope and healing to those who wear it today.

The creation of the Association of the Immaculate Heart of Mary by gentle Father Charles drew people in the thousands to the church of Our Lady of Victories, making it a national shrine. The impact of our Lady was not confined to Paris, for as the association spread to other churches, they also saw huge increases in their congregations.

La Salette in rural southeastern France is now a pilgrimage destination. The message our Lady gave to the two children focused on the conversion of all humanity to Christ and resulted in the foundation of the Missionaries of Our Lady of La Salette six years later. For us now, as for France then, our Lady gives a message of hope in dark times.

It is poignant that our Lady then revealed her message to a young victim of the industrial revolution, Bernadette. This uneducated child lived with her large family in the dark cellar of a relative's house, formerly used as a jail. Her father had lost his successful flour-milling business to the machines and could no longer afford to provide schooling for his children. From this unpromising tale of poverty and displacement, the healing properties of the waters of Lourdes draw millions of people to this day, and at that time gave believers new courage and resilience. Catholicism in secular France was back on the map, with reformed clergy, full churches, many confraternities of prayer and social action groups, and parish pilgrimages.

Louis and Zélie were married while our Lady was still appearing to Bernadette at Lourdes, so it is not surprising that the tender Mother of God was a rich source of courage, resilience, and healing to our Martin family in Alençon. Mary had central place in the heart of the home, for a statue of our Lady had been given to Louis after he returned to Alençon on completing his studies as a watchmaker. Her arms outstretched in welcome, this was the same image of Mary and Mother whose tender smile was to save his extremely ill, youngest daughter, Thérèse. Zélie and Louis held Mary in their hearts wherever she was honored, for when her brother was studying medicine in Paris, Zélie had no hesitation in asking him, "Would you like to make me happy? When you go to Madame D's house, go into Notre-Dame de Victoires and light a candle for me; this would be a help to me" (CF 6). Louis regularly went on pilgrimages to Marian sites, and his wife was later to go to Lourdes in the hope of a cure.

Jansenism

However, Mary's messages of hope and healing to a beleaguered church did not banish the pervading undercurrent of Jansenism throughout Catholic France, a distorted view of God's justice that lingers on to this day. Cornelius Jansen was a bishop of Ypres in Belgium whose life's work was a huge tome called *Augustinus* comprising his compendium of the writings of St. Augustine. He died in 1638 while writing the last chapter, but his followers took the book to Rome where it was carefully studied by theologians. From the enormous volume of material, they distilled five heretical themes that were denounced by Pope Urban VIII as going against Catholic doctrine.

Three of these heretical themes seemed to particularly influence the Catholicism of nineteenth-century Normandy: original sin, perfect contrition, and predestination. Regarding the first, Jansen thought that all human beings were "depraved" unless touched by God's grace, which could not be resisted and therefore did not require cooperation through the person's free will.

Regarding the second premise, Jansen argued that only "perfect" contrition could save a person, not just a good effort to be sorry, and no extenuating circumstances were allowed (such as stealing a loaf when starving), apart from "actual constraint." People could merit a reward in this world or the next through suffering and good works, a payment given as a remuneration of their service by a God of justice. Conversely, people or indeed nations would be punished for their misbehavior by the same God of justice.

"Perfect contrition" also controlled reception of the Eucharist. While the Jesuits encouraged Catholics to receive Communion frequently as an encouragement to holiness, Jansen's followers discouraged it, arguing that a person had to fulfill exacting requirements before being deemed worthy of receiving the Blessed Sacrament. They stipulated that a person had to be free, not only of grave (mortal) sin such as adultery, but also of venial sin such as anger, and thus were obliged to go to confession just before receiving Communion, and then request permission to receive the sacrament from their confessor.

Third, the Jansenistic premise on predestination taught that Christ died for a select few on whom he bestowed his grace; he did not die for all human beings, as the church believes and teaches. A person was thereby predestined to be saved or not but could lose that privilege through persistent and unrepentant sin.

We will see how Zélie's spirituality developed through these negative influences to a deep awareness of God's mercy and her utter dependence on him, a spirituality that was absorbed by her observant little daughter, Thérèse. Like her mother, Thérèse initially believed that suffering was the path to sanctity, but later she desired to be a victim not of God's justice but of his merciful love. She would write, "I know that Jesus cannot desire useless sufferings for us, and that He would not inspire the longings I feel [to be a victim of merciful love] unless he wanted to grant them" (S 181).

Zélie is not a pious writer, but through her descriptions of her demanding work and worries about her children she opens a chink into the impact of Jansenism on this devoutly Catholic family. Salvation was seen to be through suffering. She gave an insight into her thinking when she told God, "You know full well that I don't have time to be sick," and felt she was answered beyond all hope when, in response, God seemed to say to her, "Since you don't have time to be sick, perhaps you'll have time to suffer a lot of pain?" (CF 70). Later, she said, "Oh well, we only live to have torments of every kind. . . . I often tell myself that if I'd done half of all this [suffering] to win Heaven, I could be a canonized saint!" (CF 152). As the Prussians descended on Alençon (see chapter 6), she bemoaned, "How can it be that everyone does not recognize that this war is a punishment?" (CF 64). Even flooding in Lisieux, where her brother lived, carried a warning from God: "Sinful people are hardly benefitting from it. They would need something worse for them to open their eyes" (CF 134).

A good bookkeeper herself, Zélie's letters revealed the generally held view that this bookkeeping God of justice rewards with a gentle death and everlasting life in heaven those chosen ones who are judged worthy of salvation through their sufferings and good works. People could also be saved through the suffering and prayers of others or released from purgatory by having perhaps hundreds of masses offered for them. In her grief after the death of her father, Zélie told her sister-in-law, "We've already had three Masses said for him. We intend to request a great number of them so that, if he has anything to atone for, he'll quickly be delivered from Purgatory" (CF 38).

Lacking the infusion of baptismal grace, nonbaptized babies were consigned to limbo, a place of eternal exclusion from heaven. Hence Zélie's urgency to get her sick babies baptized and her worries about children suffering in purgatory if they had been "imperfect" before they died.

A Beleaguered Church

The Martin family benefited enormously from the revival of the church in the face of anticlericalism and the separation of church and state. The bishops of France needed to revitalize the hearts of the faithful. They supported pilgrimages to Lourdes and La Salette, set up home missions, and restored public celebrations of feast days, such as the Corpus Christi procession, a procession to honor Joan of Arc, and in Alençon, another to honor St. Catherine of Alexandria, patroness of young women and lace-makers.

As well as the special events, there was a wide range of lay organizations for Catholics to choose from, such as the Association of Prayer for the Salvation of France (joined by Zélie, her mother, and her sister); the Confraternity of the Agonizing Heart of Jesus and the Archconfraternity of Christian Mothers (joined by Zélie); the Conferences of St. Vincent de Paul; and the Nocturnal Eucharistic Adoration (both joined by Louis). Zélie was also a member of the Third Order of Franciscans that met each month at the convent of the Poor Clares. She turned often to these kind and wise sisters for advice and support throughout her marriage.

Louis would assuage his sense of helplessness at times of family crisis by going on a pilgrimage to fast and pray, for he had great faith in its power to answer prayer. Unlike our peaceful pilgrimage experiences today, a pilgrimage could take some courage, as Zélie vividly described:

> When the pilgrims returned to Alençon, there was an enormous crowd round the station and all along the road . . . the travelers were wearing all the badges from the pilgrimage [to Lourdes].
>
> My husband left first, with a little red cross attached to his chest. Several people heckled him and others laughed. But that was nothing compared to what happened next. When they saw most of the pilgrims wearing rosaries round their necks with beads as big as chestnuts, they insulted them in every way. Several were brought to the police station. However, they didn't return in a procession because the town council had forbidden it. (CF 109)

The Industrial Revolution

Louis's pilgrimages to more distant places were made possible by the late arrival of the railway in Alençon in 1853. However, trains also carried diseases that spread freely in the overcrowded and filthy houses where factory workers lived forty to fifty to one room. In this pre-antibiotic age, there were repeated outbreaks of typhoid, tuberculosis was rife, and infant mortality soared. Baby formula was yet to be invented and wet nurses for the factory women were in short supply. Sadly, babies in the care of wet nurses were even more likely to die, as Zélie herself was to discover.

One practical way of helping the young factory workers who lacked any basic amenities or family support in the industrialized towns was through the Catholic Circle, founded for this very purpose. Louis helped establish the Circle in Alençon, where the group organized concerts and shows, as Zélie described: "This evening there's a big meeting at the Catholic Circle. The young people are going to put on a very amusing little play, and the parents, along with the Circle Committee, are invited" (CF 154).

Industrial development passed Alençon by, but indirectly it had a significant impact on the economy of the town. Demand for the extremely fine Alençon lace surged due to the enriched middle classes' desire to possess this symbol of the old regime and aristocracy, and the industry profited from the mechanization of transport: the railway link to Paris and the steam liners crossing the Atlantic. *Point d'Alençon* was much sought after in the fine Parisian shops, and private purchasers came from all over Europe. However, its fabrication was slow: one piece of lace passed through eight to nine pairs of hands of individual craftswomen working at home, each specializing in a unique stitch pattern, before all the pieces were joined together to make the final article. Zélie not only assembled the lace with extraordinary skill but was also recognized as an excellent businesswoman who completed orders on time.

CONCLUSION

To answer the question at the start of this chapter, far from being removed from the world in an enclosed Catholic family haven, Louis and Zélie Martin's marriage was buffeted and shaped by the political, economic, and social events of their time. Their married life bridged the end of the Second Empire under Napoleon II and the beginning of the Third Republic. They experienced the Prussian invasion firsthand and the ongoing conflict between royalists and republicans, sandwiched between anticlericalism and Catholic revival. Through her direct interventions, our Lady became embedded in the Catholic psyche, epitomized by her intimate relationship with Louis and Zélie Martin. This man and wife of their time benefited from the expanding railways and the new markets brought by the industrial revolution, but they also anguished over the suffering of its victims.

Throughout all these destabilizing events, their one focus was to understand and do God's will, to hand their lives over to his care. This objective was firmly established in each of their hearts before they met on the bridge and was to shape the start of their marriage.

QUESTIONS FOR REFLECTION

- What influence do national or world events have on your family life? Is there a way in which our Lady can become part of prayer in your family and bring hope and comfort when threats to peace are a cause for distress and fear?

- Do you see God as judgmental or as merciful? Is there a block that prevents you from approaching God in prayer or in the sacraments?

- Do you feed yourself spiritually to enrich your married life? Is there any group in your parish that could help deepen the spiritual foundations for you and perhaps also your husband or wife?

4

An Ideal Marriage?

I will lead the blind
by a road they do not know,
by paths they have not known
I will guide them.
I will turn the darkness before them into light,
the rough places into level ground.

—Isaiah 42:16

DETOURS BEFORE WE FIND OURSELVES

Searching for Perfection

We all have ideals, ideas of perfection to which we aspire—in our careers, in our marriage, in our children, and especially in ourselves. It is natural to want to do well, to be recognized and rewarded. The problem comes when the ideal is unattainable and we feel a failure for not being perfect, or blame others for betraying the ideal image we had of them.

Saints are often perceived as spiritual superstars who have somehow achieved that ideal, who have followed a path of perfection above us ordinary mortals, so we cannot hope to reach their high standards. We feel we are too blind and imperfect, that we lack the prayerful prowess to follow in the footsteps of such holy people. Louis and Zélie show us, however, that saints are *normal* people who, in their search for God, come to understand that there exists deep within every human being a vibrant beauty that God sees in his loving gaze. It can be truly said that beauty is in the eye of the Beholder. In his lyrical poem *The Spiritual Canticle*, St. John of the Cross gives these words to the bride (the soul, or the person):

Do not despise me;
for if, before, you found me dark,
now truly you can look at me
since you have looked
and left in me grace and beauty. (C 33.2)

John goes on to explain how, under God's gaze, the soul, however "dark" it feels, is made beautiful, and the more beautiful the soul becomes, the more God gazes on the person and delights in the inner beauty. The saints are those who open their faults and failings to this healing gaze: their hidden guilt and remorse, their fear and anguish, and their addictions, loneliness, and despair. Their very *im*perfections become, under God's gaze, the doorway to perfection.

Celibacy and Virginity

Louis and Zélie each wanted to do God's will, to follow the path to perfection. Where would this lead them? The church at the time taught that the higher path to perfection was by total dedication to God's service through virginity or celibacy,[1] so this was

---

1. "If anyone saith that the marriage state is to be placed above the state of virginity, or of celibacy, and that it is not better and more blessed to remain in virginity, or in celibacy, than to be united in matrimony; let him be anathema" (Council of Trent, 1545–1563, canon 10).

the path to take. Both Louis and Zélie sought to join religious communities devoted to prayer and the service of others and, as we have seen, both were rejected and "failed" in their endeavors. Nothing daunted, Louis pursued his career as a watchmaker, finding a routine of work and prayer. In marriage also, he sought to center his life on God and searched for the most perfect way to do this. In his reading, he came across a theological text that proposed the concept of a "white marriage" or a "Josephite marriage": a marriage without any sexual relations, modeled on that of the Virgin Mary and her husband Joseph. Although the source of the full text is unknown, Louis copied a section of it into his private notebook: "The bond which constitutes this sacrament [of marriage] is independent of its consummation. . . . These marriages always have that which is essential for their validity, they even have this advantage over the others: of representing in a more perfect manner the chaste and totally spiritual union of Jesus Christ with his Church."[2] This then was the path that he resolved to take in his marriage to Zélie, a path that he understood would perfectly combine the life of the religious with that of the married person.

We do sometimes use religious motives to express our hidden and legitimate desires. Louis searched out theological support for a "white" or "Josephite marriage" so he could follow his chosen path of perfection and sanctity, by following much the same routine of work and prayer with Zélie to which he was accustomed as a bachelor. For everyone, the adjustment from carefree singleness to the sharing of life with another person is a significant step that may demand separation from family and friends, finding a new home, balancing the demands of two jobs,

2. Clapier, *Louis et Zélie Martin*, 76.

and bringing up their children. In his desire to live out his view of perfection, little did Louis know that he and Zélie would fulfill to the letter the teaching of the Catholic Church in a way that resonates with every mother and father today, and to a degree of holiness that is open to all.

At the Second Vatican Council (1962–1965) the church insisted that *all* Christians are called to perfection. This "universal call to holiness" is to be achieved or accomplished through whichever state of life one has chosen. In Vatican II's *Lumen Gentium* (Dogmatic Constitution on the Church), the church reflects its understanding of holiness for all as follows:

> Married people and Christian parents have their own path to pursue. With a love that is loyal they must give each other support in grace throughout their lives. They must steep in Christian teaching and the virtues of the gospel, the children they have lovingly received from God. This is their way of presenting all people with an example of untiring, generous love, of building the brotherhood of charity, of being outstanding witnesses to Mother Church's fertility, of co-operating in it, to show and to share the love Christ has had for his bride, the love with which he gave himself up on her behalf. (LG 41)

More recently Pope Francis clarified the concept of perfection in modern family life. In his apostolic exhortation *Amoris Laetitia* (The Joy of Love), he says, "Following a certain theological tradition, one speaks of a 'state of perfection,' this has to do not with continence in itself, but with the entirety of life based on the evangelical counsels.[3] . . . Such perfection is possible and accessible to every man and woman" (AL 160).

---

3. The evangelical counsels are poverty, chastity, and obedience.

Zélie's Dilemma

In his zeal for the ideal, Louis needed to persuade his newly wedded wife to live with him as a sister with a brother. This would not be an easy decision for Zélie. Her rejection by the Daughters of Charity in 1850 had left her shocked but undaunted; she took the rebuff as a sign from God that her destiny was to be married and have a large family, as she expressed clearly in her prayer: "Lord, since, unlike my sister, I am not worthy to be Your bride, I will enter the married state in order to fulfill Your holy will. I beg of You to give me many children and to let them all be consecrated to You."[4]

Despite her resolve to serve God in a new way through marriage and family life, there was an obstacle: Zélie's parents had no money for a dowry, an obligation in those days. Who in her social class would accept her? Being the determined young woman she was, she took the bold step of becoming self-sufficient and trained to become an artisan in Alençon lace. Now she could bring her own dowry to her wedding and start the family she so much desired.

We do not know when Louis broached the subject of remaining celibate with his new bride, but we do know something of the huge emotional turmoil it provoked in Zélie and her astounding resolve to serve God in this new and unexpected way.

FINDING THEIR WAY

Sequence of Transitions

With Élise's entrance to the Visitation convent, Zélie had lost her sister and confidante on whom she utterly depended. On top of

---

this bereavement, in three short months Zélie experienced three major revisions of her call in life: first, to be a nun; second, to be married with children; and third, to be married but remain childless. Everything came to a head when she visited her sister, whom she missed so deeply, at the convent, and found herself in floods of tears—on her wedding day! She poured her heart out and was held safe in her sister's arms, who then wrote a reassuring letter to her: "You can be tranquil about what you have told me, I will tell no one except our good Mistress [her superior]; be assured that your secret will be guarded well—she will tell no one. She is delighted that you have embraced a state so perfect. Tell M. Martin that I love him very much, I look on him as a brother."[5]

Nineteen years later, Zélie described this day in a letter to her daughter Pauline: "I went to see her for the first time [after Élise entered the convent] at the monastery on my wedding day. I can say that on that day I cried all my tears, more than I'd ever cried in my life, and more than I would ever cry again. My poor sister didn't know how to console me. . . . I compared my life to hers, and I cried even harder. . . . When I went back, I felt so sad to be in the middle of the world. I would have liked to hide my life with hers" (CF 192). How freshly she depicts the mixture of joy, grief, and confusion of that wedding day. It seems that with the best will in the world, she had to navigate major adjustments in her life far too quickly, and all without ceremony or recognition.

Zélie found herself in a state of limbo—married but not to be a mother, nun-like but not to be a religious. Her path would be unrecognized by society: she would have no ceremonies of clothing or profession to mark her progression as a nun, and no "little bundles of joy" to mark her entrance into the world of

---

5. Clapier, *Louis et Zélie Martin*, 87, from *Summerium documentorum ex officio concinnatum*, Rome, 1987. My translation.

motherhood. She would lead a semi-religious, hidden life with Louis in which their respective professions would be their full-time occupations.

Infertility

Infertility and childlessness, whether chosen or inadvertent, soon raises questions: "No children yet?" "No pitter-patter of tiny feet?" Friends have babies and become absorbed by diapers and potty training; conversations with them are across two different worlds. A woman's womb is ready for new life, but month after month she is still empty inside. Each menstrual period can bring a sense of grief. When Louis went downstairs each morning to work in his watch and jewelry shop, or climbed the steps to his pavilion to read and pray, how did Zélie cope? Was she lonely at home, with her needles and lace? Whatever her feelings at the time, nearly five years later, she was to say, "When I think of what God has done for me and my husband, God, in whom I've put all my trust and in whose hands I've put the care of my whole life, I don't doubt that His Divine Providence watches over His children with special care" (CF 1).

One thing is sure: she is a saint who understands what it is to be childless; she hears the prayers of those suffering the anguish of this experience. Paradoxically, a few months later Louis and Zélie were temporary parents to a small child, one of twelve siblings whose mother had died, a young boy whom they took into their home to help the struggling father. Perhaps this little boy gave them a taste for parenting for, after ten months of married abstinence, Louis accepted the advice of his confessor to be open to the gift of children and make love to his wife.

This was a very personal conversation with a priest about which we have, for obvious reasons, no details, but it does indicate the respect Louis had for his confessor and his open-ness to hearing God's will through the ordinary means available to him within the church. He and Zélie could move on with a clear conscience to the next stage of their marriage and become a family. Zélie was overjoyed, a joy that never left her and burst forth fourteen years later, just before she gave birth to her last child, Thérèse: "As for me, I'm crazy about children; I was born to have them" (CF 83). Now was her motherhood to begin; the empty house would become a thriving home.

THE EXPERIENCE OF PARENTHOOD

Aiming for perfection

All expectant parents have ideas of how to parent before the children arrive. They attend prenatal groups, read baby-care books, and prepare the nursery. They want to give their children a chance for happiness and not repeat any perceived wrongs they suffered in their own childhoods. Certainly, Zélie was deter-mined not to give her own children the experience of feeling as she did as a child, "as sad as a shroud," as she explained: "But when we had our children, our ideas changed somewhat. We lived only for them. They were all our happiness and we never found any except in them. In short, nothing was too difficult, and the world was no longer a burden to us" (CF 192).

Did Zélie try to resist the social pressure of her society to be a "supermom," an ideal portrayed these days in glossy magazines? For her as for us, being the perfect parent has inherent cultural contradictions. Working mothers are critiqued for being selfish in pursuing their own careers and not spending enough time with their children, while homemakers are criticized for not earning money in meaningful employment and thereby failing to provide good role models for their children. A hardworking mother herself, Zélie would be overwhelmed by the demands of her business, and both she and Louis would be torn to emotional shreds by concerns for their children.

True, the survival of our children is now so much more assured than it was in Louis and Zélie's time in the nineteenth century, but there are new dangers for parents to navigate as children grow up: mobile phone addiction, seductive selfies and sexting, cyber bullying, internet pornography, gambling. How can these bourgeois French parents be of any help to us today? They inspire us not so much through their "perfect" parenting but more through their ongoing challenges and crises concerning their children, with their work-life balance and with their approach to the life-threatening situations in the world around them. They are appropriate saints for modern parents.

Transition to Parenthood

The start to their family life was wonderful, for the first two children, Marie and Pauline, more than satisfied Zélie's ideal of herself as a good mother. They were full of fun, admired by the townsfolk, and quick to learn, as she says in a letter to her brother: "Oh! I admit I don't regret being married. If you had seen the two older ones today, how pretty they looked, everyone admiring them and could not take their eyes off of them. And me, I was there beaming. I said to myself, 'They're mine!'" (CF 13).

The first baby changes life forever. I will never again be responsible just for myself. This tiny, utterly dependent human being will control my sleeping, my working, my relationship with my spouse, and my relationship with my parents. However well prepared parents are for their baby's arrival into this world, the child comes as not only a delight but also a shock, and it is understandable that many mothers feel tearful, exhausted, and anxious for some time after the baby is born. This experience of "baby blues" is so common as to be considered normal, but for some, postpartum depression descends on a new mom like a heavy weight that lasts much longer. Just as Zélie and Louis thrived with the support of their family, friends, and parish, every new mother and father in our own society needs the buttress of grandparents, friends, baby groups, and others in caring for their precious but demanding new baby.

The Role of the Church

The burgeoning Martin family was integral to their Catholic parish in Alençon, the town where they had put down roots. Their church was a place of belonging, with its fraternities and societies, missions and homilies, and above all, the source of the Eucharist and a place of prayer. In our day we can ask ourselves, do young parents in our parishes feel welcomed with new infants, or are they beset with anxiety that the baby will make a noise, produce a smelly diaper, or throw up on the church carpet? Unlike the Martin family, new parents in our own parishes may be isolated in tiny family units distant from willing grandparents and friends. Our support for them is of infinitesimal value, for holiness does not happen in isolation.

A Joyful Start

Louis and Zélie were now bursting with life. Their path to having a family had taken them along several detours before they found themselves in parenthood and deepened their roots in Alençon. Zélie told her brother, "I'm always so happy with him [Louis], he makes my life very pleasant" (CF 1). Regarding Pauline (aged eighteen months) she says, "She hugs us every minute without our telling her to do so, and she sends kisses to Jesus. . . . In other words, she's an ideal child. . . . Right now she is sitting next to me on the desk and doesn't want to leave me alone, so what I'm writing is all crooked" (CF 1, 2).

Both parents loved spending time with these little ones, Louis in the garden, Zélie at home, sometimes at a cost to her sleep: "I enjoyed myself [playing with the children and their new toys] like a child playing a game of Patience, and I paid for my childishness. I had to make a very urgent order of lace, and, to make up for lost time, I stayed up until one o'clock in the morning" (CF 21). With a 5:30 start for Mass the next morning, there was not much sleep to be had that night!

WHEN THINGS GO WRONG

For Louis and Zélie, the political and social upheavals of their time, the tribulations of the church, and the prevailing Jansenistic emphasis on a "destiny to suffer" were now alleviated by joy and fun with the children, delightful walks in the countryside, relaxing fishing in the rivers and lakes, travel on the recently built railways, and even working and dealing with employees. Common sense and humor were the leaven that expanded all aspects of their family life. But as Zélie wryly pointed out, good times don't last. Crises in their home and in their nation were on the horizon, but these would steadily deepen rather than weaken Louis and Zélie's total trust in God. Job famously said, "Naked I came from my mother's womb, and naked shall I return there; the Lord gave, and the Lord has taken away; blessed be the name of the Lord" (Job 1:20–21). These parents would be steadily stripped of their ideal images and plunged into a place of insecurity and deprivation where they had no power to "earn" anything from God.

This couple is showing us that in their ordinary family life, different in detail but not in principle from our own family lives, their experiences resonate with ours and speak to us today. Through their apparent detours in their struggle to "get it together," the Holy Spirit was quietly preparing them for a parenthood that could reach into the deepest cracks and crevices of future suffering parents and penetrate their pain with healing and peace.

From their pre-marriage ideals, Louis and Zélie were given a new heart that embraced marriage with children. Their fullness of joy from the first two healthy girls born to them would progress to times of emptiness and loss as further children suffered and died, and work overwhelmed Zélie's days. The next stage of their journey through the sacrament of marriage was to begin.

QUESTIONS FOR REFLECTION

- Are there detours in your life before marriage that you now regret? Can you, with grace from the sacraments, view these life experiences as enriching your relationship with your husband or wife rather than impoverishing it?

- Are you trying to be a supermom or superdad? Do you feel that your children's happiness is all up to you? In what way are you open to God's help in raising the family he has created and given to you and your spouse?

- How have the struggles and challenges in your married life deepened your faith and increased your resilience? What can you do to open yourself to God's loving care in the places where you feel most helpless?

5

Birth and Death, Infancy and Old Age

Louis and Zélie were married for nineteen years and one month.

—JULY 12, 1858–AUGUST 28, 1877

Births	Year	Deaths
	1859	September 9: Zélie's mother, age 54
February 22: Marie	1860	
September 7: Pauline	1861	
June 3: Léonie	1863	
October 13: Hélène	1864	
	1865	June 26: Louis's father, age 88
September 20: Joseph-Louis	1866	
December 19: Joseph-Jean-Baptiste	1867	February 14: Joseph-Louis

Continued

Births	Year	Deaths
February 24: Jeanne Guérin (niece)	1868	August 24: Joseph-Jean-Baptiste September 3: Zélie's father, age 79
April 28: Céline	1869	
August 16: Mélanie-Thérèse August 22: Marie Guérin (niece)	1870	February 22: Hélène October 8: Mélanie-Thérèse
	1871	October 16: Paul Guérin, (nephew), stillborn
January 2: Thérèse	1873	
	1877	February 24: Zélie's sister, age 48 August 28: Zélie, age 45

So I went down to the potter's house, and there he was working at his wheel. The vessel he was making of clay was spoiled in the potter's hand, and he reworked it into another vessel, as seemed good to him. . . . Just like the clay in the potter's hand, so are you in my hand, O house of Israel.

—Jeremiah 18:3–6

THE REALITY OF PARENTING

Nothing is thrown away or wasted; anything "spoiled" is reworked to form a beautiful and useful vessel made from the clay of our daily lives. God likens himself to an ordinary potter in his care for us ordinary people. He does not reject our "mistakes," our losses, and our "failures," to be thrown into oblivion to dry off and become hard lumps, but he reintegrates them into the forming clay, always kept moist and pliable in his creative gaze, always turning on the wheel of life, always being shaped by his hands.

Loss can be an experience of such pain that it is too unbearable to even think about; so it is pushed down out of conscious memory, "out of sight, out of mind." It may be loss of a parent, a sibling, or a friend; loss of a home or a job; or loss of personal integrity, status, or role. But for a mother and father, the most unnatural and insupportable loss is the death of their child, life of their life prematurely cut short.

We will see how Louis and Zélie Martin coped as their family life encompassed births and deaths, sickness and good health, joys and great sorrows. Whether deeply wondrous or totally traumatic, how did they integrate these prevalent experiences into their marriage? We will begin at the beginning.

Proud Parents

"It's the first time that I've come home for a baptism, but not the last!" exclaimed Louis, the proud dad of his "diamond" as he called Marie, his firstborn. Louis and Zélie embarked with great joy on the ship of parenthood, producing four children in just over four and a half years. After her period of waiting to get pregnant, Zélie suffered the common anxiety of first-time mothers, as when she sympathized with her pregnant sister-in-law: "I also was sick with my first little girl. I believed that all was lost, and I cried, I who so wanted a baby!" (CF 21). She seems to have carried these first three children, given birth to them, nurtured them, and continued working in her lace business with her customary energy and determination.

As the babies grew into toddlers, Zélie reveled in her "very cute" little girls and enjoyed describing their progress in speaking, in taking their first steps, and in all their delightful ways. Referring to nineteen-month-old Pauline, she says, "Believe me, she already loves to dress up. When we tell her that we're going out, she runs quickly to the closet where her most beautiful dress is and extends her little face saying, 'Wash me.' I find all this marvelous, as if it weren't perfectly natural" (CF 2).

This proud mother gives vivid cameos of her children's antics, revealing how she found herself transformed into the happy child she had never been: the deprived little girl who was never given so much as a doll. She loved to be like a child herself, to share her children's games and open their new toys with them, storing in her heart their innocent pronouncements of childish wisdom. Truly, as Zélie demonstrates in her evocative imagery, parenthood gives the opportunity to relive childhood and heal the pain of the past.

Good times cannot last, as Zélie wryly told her brother, and these dedicated parents of time past and time present would now experience the pains and losses faced by so many parents today.

Babies in Peril

Having successfully nurtured her first three babies, Zélie could not breastfeed her fourth child, Hélène, and stoically told her brother, "This baby will go to a wet nurse, unfortunately, since I'm unable to nurse the baby myself anymore. It's in God's hands" (CF 8). Louis was meticulous in finding a wet nurse of good repute, but putting their newborn baby into the care of a stranger for the first time, especially a person who lived several miles outside Alençon,[1] was a heartrending experience. Marie, then aged five and a half, remembered vividly the anguish felt by her and her mom of leaving behind her baby sister after a visit. In her *Memoirs* she wrote, "I can still see Mama kissing little Hélène before leaving. And I said to myself, 'How much it pains me to leave my little sister! How unhappy Mama must be! Poor Mama! But why doesn't she take her with us?"[2] Zélie told her brother, "I want you to know, I miss her terribly. I think of her all the time" (CF 11). How she longed to bring her new infant home and possess her completely. Fortunately, this temporary fostering had a successful outcome, and after twelve long months Hélène returned home a healthy baby.

Temporary loss of a child to a foster mother moved inexorably on to permanent loss with the death of the next two babies while in the care of wet nurses, both boys and both named Joseph. Joseph-Louis was just five months old when he died, Joseph-Jean-Baptiste was eight months old.

Zélie put all her hopes in her first beautiful boy, initially so big and strong. He was born September 20, 1866. She and Louis found him a healthy and caring wet nurse called Rose Taillé, who lived in a small village, Semallé, five miles outside Alençon. A strong child, Joseph-Louis thrived in his surrogate family, but Zélie longed for him so much that she brought him home for New Year's Day just to have that special day with him. She describes dressing him "like a prince" and delighting in carrying

---

1. Care of infants by wet nurses for a year or more was commonplace in France for the bourgeoisie, and with the arrival of mechanization, factory girls were also forced to use them.

2. *Memoirs of Sister Marie of the Sacred Heart*, written in 1909 at the request of Mother Agnès of Jesus (Pauline), in Martin and Martin, *A Call to a Deeper Love*, 11n46.

him around and hearing him laugh. What joy the entire family had with him at home! But the time came to carry a hungry little Joseph-Louis back through the frozen midwinter fields to Rose to be nursed.

Sadly, an urgent message at five o'clock the next morning found Zélie and Louis again treading the icy lanes in the dark to Rose's cottage, to see him covered in the rash of erysipelas (a streptococcal skin infection) from which he would die a month later. To add insult to injury, Zélie was blamed in the town for his death because she had taken him to Alençon when the weather was too cold. What a turnaround! Her dreams and hopes for this little boy were shattered. As was common in all Catholic families at the time, she had hopes that their first son would be a priest and was already designing in her mind some fine Alençon lace to decorate his ordination vestments.

Ten months later, the second Joseph was born on December 19, 1867, but had a rough start to life. He was sickly after a difficult delivery: "I had a terrible time and the baby was in greatest danger. For four hours I suffered the most severe pain I've ever felt" (CF 23). This poor baby never fully lived; he was so "writhing in pain" from the day he was born that the wet nurse (Rose Taillé again) was afraid to take him back with her in case he died. Zélie was very concerned for him: "He's always sleeping and hardly ever cries. I'm longing to see him very much because I'm in constant fear ever since the tragedy of his little brother" (CF 24). Seemingly at death's door, he appeared to recover from a severe episode of bronchitis, but this was a premature hope. His condition deteriorated, as she described: "I went to see him twice a day. In the morning I left at five o'clock and in the evening at eight o'clock, and I always returned with a heart filled with anguish" (CF 32).

After five months she brought him home to care for him herself, but within only three months he died of bronchitis and enteritis.[3] At least his sisters were with him for that time, and Marie, in her *Memoirs*, gives a joyous insight about her baby brother: "To make him laugh, I danced with you [Pauline] and with Léonie and Hélène too I believe, on a bed across from his cradle. We broke the bed frame. He had bursts of laughter. . . . I never saw such a jewel."[4]

April 28, 1869, brought the new life of spring and the seventh baby, Céline. Zélie had now lost all confidence that this baby (she was hoping for another boy) would live, as she explained to her sister-in-law: "So, you can't imagine how frightened I am of the future, about this little person that I'm expecting. It seems to me that the fate of the last two children will be his fate, and it is a never-ending nightmare for me. I believe the dread is worse than the misfortune. . . . The fear, for me, is torture" (CF 45).

For Céline, Louis found a wet nurse who lived locally but then transferred her to another wet nurse in the town. This woman, although of good reputation and very orderly and clean, aroused Louis's suspicions, for he would pace up and down outside her spic-and-span house listening for his baby daughter. When he eventually heard her fitful cries, he entered the house and found her abandoned in her cradle. The nurse had gone to the local bar for a drink! He immediately

---

3. In children, rotavirus is the most common cause of severe enteritis, transmitted by contaminated water or unpasteurized milk. It causes vomiting and diarrhea, with rapid dehydration in babies, and is still a major cause of hospital admissions.

4. *Memoirs of Sister Marie*, in Martin and Martin, *A Call to a Deeper Love*, 36n96.

questioned the neighbors and was shocked to learn that she was often drunk and did not feed her charges sufficiently. Louis thereby saved the life of his tiny daughter who would have died of neglect. After that the starving baby was taken to a third wet nurse, Madame Georges, also in Semallé, where Céline pulled through but not without long-term consequences for her health.

Zélie so much wanted to nurse her next baby, Marie-Melanie-Thérèse: "I kept her with me for four days and tried to breastfeed her. Unfortunately, this wasn't sufficient and we had to make her drink from a bottle.[5] The third day she came down with such an upset stomach that the doctor told me we didn't have an hour to lose, that we had to find her a wet nurse right away" (CF 59). There was no time for the ninety-minute walk to Rose Taillé's cottage so Louis and Zélie resorted to another wet nurse with good credentials who was more conveniently located in Alençon.

Melanie-Thérèse took to the wet nurse's breastfeeding and survived this crisis—but not for long, for this wet nurse also neglected her charge and Melanie-Thérèse died of starvation in only seven weeks. It was ten-year-old Marie who, on a visit with the household maid, Louise, observed that her weak and silent baby sister was famished after being belatedly nursed, and, ignoring Louise's advice to keep quiet, blurted this out at the next family meal. Zélie immediately went to bring Melanie-Thérèse home, but she was too weak to recover and soon died, leaving her mother devastated: "With each new loss, it always seems to me that I love the child I'm losing more than the others. . . . Oh! I would like to die, too!" (CF 60).

---

5. The bottle would have contained unpasteurized milk and water.

THE REALITY OF LOSS

Wet Nurses

Zélie needed wet nurses at a time when they were in huge demand by factory-working mothers and before there was any national regulation of their pay and conditions.[6] "Breast is best" was as true then as it is today, but

> by the eighteenth century the custom of sending babies away to be wet-nursed had crossed class lines, as economic conditions forced even the urban working class to place their babies with rural families for up to four years. Workers' wages were so low during this era, and rents so high that even mothers with infants had to work. Although working women were by no means novel in France, they posed a unique problem in an urban setting. No longer able to keep their infants at their sides as they toiled, working-class urban mothers began to send their babies to the countryside to be cared for by women even poorer than themselves. The custom was so pervasive among all classes that cities like Paris and Lyon literally became cities without babies. The ubiquitous custom of wet-nursing did not wane in France until World War I.[7]

Urban working mothers could not easily visit their babies staying with wet nurses miles out in the countryside and were thereby vulnerable to feeling a lack of bonding with their babies. However, throughout each forced separation, Zélie and

---

6. The Roussel Law in 1874 (a year after Thérèse of Lisieux was born) mandated that every infant placed with a paid guardian outside the parents' home be registered with the state.

7. Jacqueline H. Wolf, "Wet-Nursing," Encyclopedia of Children and Childhood in History and Society, 2008, accessed October 14, 2016, *http://www.faqs.org/childhood/Th-W/wet-nursing*

Louis, and indeed the older girls, kept the flame of love alive in their hearts and their minds for the absent child. They went to great effort to walk miles in all kinds of weather to maintain contact and were delighted when it seemed that their gorgeous cherub recognized them. Zélie anguished over her inability to feed her babies herself, as she put in her succinct way: "I often think of the mothers who have the joy of feeding their children themselves. As for me, I have to see them all die one after the other!" (CF 87).

In mid-nineteenth-century France, more than one in three infants died, usually of infection, so although each loss was heartrending, it was not unusual, and the infant death rate in the Martin household would have been average for a family at the time. However, Zélie was pregnant with her eighth baby when the unexpected happened. Five-year-old Hélène died on Marie's tenth birthday on February 22, 1870. She had had measles a year earlier, but the cause of her death is not known. What we do know is that after being "accustomed to seeing her suffer" (from fever), Zélie tormented herself for failing to notice that Hélène was getting steadily weaker, and then blamed herself further for giving her bread soup, for she died the next day in her arms. Zélie pours out to her brother: "When he [Louis] came home and saw his poor little daughter dead, he began to sob, crying, 'My little Hélène! My little Hélène!' Then together we offered her to God. And now I'm left with the bitter remorse of having given her something to eat. My dear brother, do you think that this made her die?" (CF 52).

Bereavement

With the death of their little "angels," Melanie-Thérèse and the two Josephs, Louis and Zélie were sad but not over-whelmed. Encouraged by her sister in the convent, Zélie said

she *tried very hard* to put everything in the hands of God and
to be abandoned to his will, although this effort in faith did
not prevent her experiencing grief for her infants. The death
of Hélène was a different matter, a shock that devastated both
parents, and Zélie came near to losing the will to live. Feeling
unwell herself with daily fever, headaches, and exhaustion, she
writes, "Sometimes I imagine that I'll go away as gently as my
little Hélène. I assure you that I barely care for my own life.
Ever since I lost this child, I feel a burning desire to see her
again" (CF 54).

Time moved on, and Zélie did not lock herself up in self-
recrimination and grief but allowed it to become a vehicle of
empathy toward her sister-in-law, Céline Guérin, whose third
child was stillborn. She tried to console her by assuring her that
her baby was at God's side and could see her and love her, but
this positive stance was an effort proportionate to her sorrow,
for she was deeply affected herself.

These days losing a stillborn child[8] is thankfully less common than it was in nineteenth-century rural France, but the loss
of a child through miscarriage[9] is much more common than we
realize and secretly affects many women and their husbands.
This loss is more desolating for older women who are less likely
to become pregnant again. Zélie was also aware that, in her for-
ties, her time for giving birth was running out. In sympathizing

8. Stillbirth is defined in the UK as a pregnancy ending after twenty-four
weeks, and in the U.S. as one ending after twenty weeks. One in every two hundred births ends in a stillbirth. See "Stillbirth," NHS Choices, accessed October
14, 2016, *http://www.nhs.uk/conditions/stillbirth/*.

9. In the UK, it is estimated that one in eight known pregnancies ends
in a miscarriage, depending on the age of the mother. See "Miscarriage," NHS
Choices, accessed October 14, 2016, *http://www.nhs.uk/conditions/miscarriage/*.

with her sister-in-law, she described her own pain at closing the eyes of her dead children but said she had no regret for the sorrows and problems she had endured for them. She strongly refuted the notion expressed (and spread) by well-meaning people that it would have been better not to give birth to them. Zélie knew they were born for a purpose and, after death, were the source of "extraordinary grace," for they had already answered her prayer for Hélène when she had a severe ear infection. Her children in heaven were part of her life: "You see, my dear sister, it's a very good thing to have little angels in Heaven, but it's no less painful to lose them" (CF 72).

As a lay Franciscan, Zélie regularly went to see the Poor Clare nuns for spiritual guidance, prayer, and support. Through their lives of prayer, the sisters transmitted a relationship with God that was beyond spoken prayers and more profound than external piety. In the face of relentless loss, the prayerful accompaniment by these sisters would have surely helped to lift the couple above a state of despondency. Even so, there were times when the losses seemed overwhelming. In October 1871, Zélie could write to her brother after his wife's stillbirth, "For our own good, He may allow us to suffer a great deal, but never without His help and His grace" (CF 71), but in May 1875, she would say, "You see, at the moment, life seems so heavy for me to bear, and I don't have the courage because everything looks black to me" (CF 132).

What brought about such a change in her usual composure in the face of illness and death over the four intervening years between these two letters? Zélie's determination to trust in God could not suppress her natural feelings, her fear brought about by the cumulative effect of illness and death in her family. Children in those days were at risk of death from common infections:

measles, whooping cough, typhoid, tuberculosis. Céline, often ill and frail in physique, caused her mother to dread that she would slip away like Hélène; the third sister, Léonie, suffered from purulent eczema as a baby and later nearly died from measles with fits; and at the age of thirteen, Marie was at death's door over several months with typhoid fever. Their father gave as much practical help as he could but, in his helplessness and distress, would resort to prayer. This often took the form of a pilgrimage and fasting, sometimes on foot, to seek a cure from Our Lady or a saint for his sick child.

In addition to concerns for her children, Zélie was devastated when her beloved brother Isidore moved from Alençon to Lisieux in 1868 to set up his pharmacy business there, as she told him in no uncertain terms: "But here is another reason to be sad: you want to move seventy leagues [about 170 miles] from here! . . . So, I'll say goodbye to you forever; we'll hardly see each other until the next world because, never in my poor life, which, I believe, will not be long, will I have the time to go see you. As for you, you won't have any more time than I'll have" (CF 15).

The stillbirth of her brother's much-wanted son was another shock that brought a resurgence of grief for Zélie's own dead babies and Hélène. Around the same time, an acute fear of impending loss came about her sister, Élise, who was gradually dying from tuberculosis and had suffered a frightening episode of breathing difficulty. Always close to the "holy one" as she teasingly called her, Zélie felt she would lose everything if she lost her. But there were also others in the family for her and Louis to worry about: the older generation.

Gendarmerie in Saint-Denis-sur-Sarthon, where Zélie lived as a child

Louis Martin's house
and watchmaker's shop,
15, rue du Pont Neuf,
Alençon (today no. 35)

The Pavilion, Alençon

The Crystal Palace, London, site of the 1851 International Exhibition where Alençon lace was exhibited

St Leonard's Bridge, Alençon

The Town Hall, Alençon, where Louis and Zélie had their civil marriage on July 12, 1858 (preceding the Catholic ceremony, according to custom)

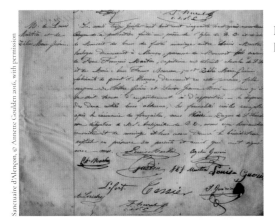

Marriage certificate of Louis and Zélie Martin

Zélie's work desk (to the left of the mantelpiece)

Stained-glass window depicting the baptism of St. Thérèse, in the baptism chapel of Notre-Dame Basilica, Alençon

Notre-Dame Basilica, Alençon, where Louis and Zélie were married on July 13, 1858

Louis and Zélie's house, rue Saint-Blaise, Alençon

Moïse and Rose Taillé's cottage at Semallé

Chapel of Bon
Sauveur hospital,
Caen

Alençon lace

Alençon lace made by Zélie

Château de la Musse, Evreux

Les Buissonnets, Lisieux

OLD AND YOUNG

Sandwich Generation

We speak these days of the "sandwich generation": couples who care for not only their own small children but also their elderly parents. It is described as a modern phenomenon, but Louis and Zélie give us a prime example from the nineteenth century. Zélie was very supportive of her husband's parents, especially her mother-in-law who was the caregiver for Louis's father in the last three years of his life. Although her father-in-law died "like a saint," Zélie was traumatized, saying, "I would never have believed that this could have such an effect on me. I'm shattered" (CF 14). When she saw him laid out, "his arms so stiff and his face so cold," the reality of death seemed to hit home. There were no pious utterances; her shock was not even softened by her belief in heaven, for she admitted, "I confess, death terrifies me" (CF 14). Here again, Zélie revealed how faith and trust in God did not protect her from feeling shock and fear, nor was she ashamed to admit it.

After his wife died, Zélie's own father lived with the Martin family, but when his house down the road became available (it had been occupied by tenants), he decided he would move back. This veteran military man was stubborn in his determination, but Zélie was more stubborn, concerned that he could not manage on his own. She and Louis joined in begging him to stay with them, not by telling him that he was unable to care for himself, but by explaining that she needed him around as he was a great help to her. A smart move!

Louis and Zélie demonstrate in action the view of our present-day Pope Francis, who emphasizes the important role grandparents have in our families, in *Amoris Laetitia* (The Joy of Love): "Their words, their affection or simply their presence help children realize that history did not begin with them, and that they are now part of an age-old pilgrimage and that they need to respect all that came before them" (AL 192).

Looking at the marriage timeline above, the sickness and deaths of these much-loved military grandfathers are intertwined with the deaths of Louis and Zélie's children: Louis's father died two years before Joseph-Louis, and Zélie's father died ten days after Joseph-Jean-Baptiste. Zélie had a close bond with her father who evidently enjoyed being a granddad and regaled the family with stories of his Napoleonic exploits.

Although increasingly dependent, Zélie's father was a rock of strength for her. Her grief after his death speaks to our hearts: "Saturday I looked everywhere for my father, it seemed to me that I was going to find him. I couldn't imagine that I was going to be separated from him forever" (CF 39). She describes the first stage of grief perfectly: searching and denial. Then she felt numb and couldn't pray either at his grave or at that of her "two little angels," and was shocked to find herself "seeming to be indifferent." She visited the cemetery every Sunday, where she felt her father was following her and seemed to be suffering.

New Life

On January 2, 1873, into this valley of death came a bright and vibrant new life, that of Zélie's last child, Thérèse. Zélie initially succeeded in feeding her with the bottle for ten marvelous weeks before Thérèse too contracted the dreaded baby killer, enteritis. She was at death's door when Rose Taillé was rushed to the scene and again saved a Martin baby's life with the flow of milk from her breasts. She took the new baby to her home to live with her husband and four small children. Zélie was bereft once more, saying, "But my poor little one has left. It's very sad to have raised a child for two months and then to have to entrust her to strangers' hands. What consoles me is knowing that God wants it this way, since I did everything I could to raise her myself. So I have nothing to reproach myself for in this regard" (CF 89). Thérèse blossomed in the freedom and fresh air of the countryside and naturally bonded to Rose as her mother figure. Much more comfortable with country women, this robust toddler did not take kindly to being separated from her surrogate mother and siblings when she returned to Alençon at thirteen months of age (April 2, 1874); she cried inconsolably. But Thérèse soon became closely attached to her mother and inseparable from her sister nearest in age, Céline. Zélie explained, "Thérèse is beginning to say everything. She's becoming cuter and cuter, but that's not a little problem, I assure you, because she's continually at my side, and it's difficult for me to work" (CF 118). "She babbles from morning 'til night. She sings us little songs" (CF 124). One could say she was the life and soul of the Martin household.

Nurturing the Soul

We see here a Catholic couple who depended not on their own strength but on food for the soul in the Eucharist, for they regularly went to the 5:30 a.m. weekday Mass for working folk. Louis and Zélie were also faithful to religious devotions such as vespers and Benediction of the Blessed Sacrament; they enjoyed being part of their parish community; and most important of all, were united with their family in prayer every evening.

In line with the Jansenistic view of God as a God of justice, they initially had a vision of life on earth as being a time of exile from their real home in heaven, with an assurance of eternal life contingent upon good works, sacrifice, and penance in this world. There was thereby a sense of *control* over God's reward system. If individuals behaved well, God would give them a just reward, but if a person or even a nation failed to follow God's commands, God would punish them through suffering and disaster. Even Zélie was prey to this way of thinking: "I learned about the flood in Lisieux. . . . As you say, my dear sister, all of this is quite dreadful. This is a great curse, but sinful people are hardly benefitting from it. They would need something worse for them to open their eyes" (CF 134).

Steadily, however, not only was Louis and Zélie's human logic of *earning* the reward of heavenly joy gradually transformed into faith-filled trust, but also any anesthetic effect from belief in heavenly joys to come was overwhelmed by the raw pain of seeing those they had loved and nurtured suffer and die. They did not detach themselves from their painful experiences but entered as fully as any human being can into them, so that these experiences were integrated into the vessels they were to become. They discovered God's nurturing presence in the very darkness of their beings. Talking about her fears for her yet unborn Céline, Zélie says, "This morning, during Mass, I had such dark thoughts about this that I was very deeply moved. The best thing to do is to put everything in the hands of God and await the outcome in peace and abandonment to His will. That's what I'm going to try very hard to do" (CF 45). When her brother Isidore's wholesale drug business was destroyed by fire, Zélie wrote in sympathy to her sister-in-law, "One must have a great deal of faith and resignation to accept this setback without complaint and with submission to God's will. . . . My dear sister, you've already begun to see that life is not a bed of roses. God wills this to detach us from the world and raise our thoughts toward heaven" (CF 90). No longer was misfortune a punishment; rather it was the gentle hands of the Potter using every lump of clay to form a beautiful vessel, shaping the human being in his own image and likeness. We say that severe misfortune can make or break a marriage. Pope Francis calls this "the challenge of crises":

> "The life of every family is marked by all kind of crises, yet, these are also part of its dramatic beauty. . . . Each crisis becomes an apprenticeship in growing closer together or learning a little more about what it means to be married. There is no need for couples to resign themselves to an inevitable downward spiral or a tolerable mediocrity. On the contrary, when marriage is seen as a challenge that involves overcoming obstacles, each crisis becomes an opportunity to let the wine of their relationship age and improve." (AL 232)

God uses the events that could break a marriage to strengthen it and even bring a new channel of happiness. How can this happen? Pope Francis gives a simple answer: "Crises need to be faced together. . . . Communication is an art learned in moments of peace in order to be practiced in moment of difficulty" (AL 234). Communication is the key, and this can take courage. We hold back, wondering to ourselves, "Will I be understood, am I being silly, will my husband/wife be upset?" But if we can be open with each other in small things, as Zélie was, we are in a stronger position to face crises together without blaming ourselves or others.

Louis and Zélie allowed their grief and sorrow to lead not into bitterness, regret, or self-blame but into a deeper awareness of God as a loving Father. They show us how the realization of our vulnerability and helplessness opens us to God's longing to be beside us, even deep within us, at our times of turmoil and anguish. In his commentary on *The Spiritual Canticle*, St. John of the Cross puts it in his own lyrical way: "Suffering is the means of [the soul] penetrating further, deep into the thicket of the delectable wisdom of God. The purest suffering brings with it the purest and most intimate knowing, and consequently the purest and highest joy, because it is a knowing from further within" (C 36.12).

What was Zélie's impact on the future saint Thérèse of Lisieux? This little girl had but a short time with her mother, but in those few early years she was attached to her as if by an invisible piece of string, ensuring that this most precious human being in her life was there for her. "This little one is by my side. . . . Sunday I took her to Vespers, and she didn't leave me alone, so we're only going to go to Benediction." Later in the same letter to Pauline, she writes, "I hear the baby calling, 'Mama' while coming down the stairs. At each step she says 'Mama!' and if I don't answer every time, she remains there without moving forward or backward" (CF 146).

Without needing words, Thérèse keenly observed her mama's relationship with God and was as determined as a feisty three-year-old can be to go with her to church whenever she was allowed. While both parents certainly taught her how to say her prayers and count her good deeds, perhaps more influential on the future saint was this wordless witness of her mother's own "little way" of mundane sufferings and joys that was leading her away from the God of retribution and toward a God of mercy and love.

These dedicated parents were being molded by the Potter into union with him through their ordinary family life. They have been recognized by the Catholic Church as saints, not because they produced a child who became a Doctor of the Church, but because, by living out parenthood to its deepest depths, they allowed themselves to be formed into splendid vessels by the gently creative hand of God.

QUESTIONS FOR REFLECTION

- What do you enjoy doing with children? Are you able to enter their world and be a child again, thus reliving and, if necessary, healing your own childhood memories?

- Do you have some worst fears for members of your own family? Do you keep these to yourself, or are you able to share them with your spouse, or someone else who understands?

- Have you had experience of a miscarriage or a stillborn child, your own or that of a family member or friend? How has grief been acknowledged and the child remembered? How does your faith in God the Father's care keep that child as part of the family?

6

Work and Wealth

My life is but a weaving
Between my God and me.
I cannot choose the colors
He weaveth steadily.

Oft' times He weaveth sorrow;
And I in foolish pride
Forget He sees the upper
And I the underside.

Not 'til the loom is silent
And the shuttles cease to fly
Will God unroll the canvas
And reveal the reason why.

—SOURCE UNKNOWN

WORK

Bricks and Stitches of Life

Our lives can be likened to building a wall or knitting a blanket: to reach the desired outcome a series of small repetitive events must take place. Brick by brick or stitch by stitch, the work seems painstakingly slow. From the back, it looks plain and knobby, but the front, with varied patterns appropriate for different stages in the construction, emerges over time as a beautifully crafted piece of work. In this hidden way, God involves himself in our lives, each day another row of bricks or stitches made from the events of the day, each year 365 rows. . . . And how many rows will complete the picture? We do not know when the work of our lives will be finished, but we know that all these *small things* have the power to work together in completing the fascinating, intricate, and extraordinarily beautiful individual that God sees deep within every man, woman, and child he has created.

Those who work with families will tell you how important it is for people to "pick up" lost stitches (or missing bricks) in their lives—perhaps an estranged daughter needs to be hugged, or a new "unwanted" baby be welcomed. A couple may find renewed harmony in unraveling a piece of life from the past and knitting it back into the whole, perhaps by bridging a long-standing family rift or by releasing a festering secret.

The great discovery is that, although seemingly insignificant, each individual stitch is integral and vital to the whole— our approach to the little things becomes the fabric of our approach to the whole of life. The little struggles to hold back an unkind word, to refrain from criticism, and the hidden efforts to respond kindly to an unwanted demand on our time and energy—each of these get knitted into the pattern that eventually emerges on the front. It is tempting to see the big sacrifices and offerings as the actions that give us value, but these miniscule moments are the seedbed of goodness.

Zélie and Louis Martin lived their family life to the full. They can show us how, stitch by stitch and brick by brick, they built an inspiring, *normal*, and workaday arrangement called married life, all the while recognizing God's involvement. St. John of the Cross likens God to a stonemason who gradually chips away at a block of marble to release the beautiful image hidden in the pearlescent rock. Initially, the craftsman uses hefty strokes of the hammer on his chisel to hew out large chunks; then he picks up a very fine chisel and uses small and delicate taps to shape the fine features of his unique masterpiece. St. John speaks from experience when he says in his *Counsels*, "Some will chisel with words, telling you what you would rather not hear; others by deed, doing against you what you would rather not endure; others by temperament, being in their person and in their actions a bother and annoyance to you; and others by their thoughts, neither esteeming nor feeling love for you" (Co 3). Marriage is the means by which God does just that with each one of us, through our broken relationships, our daily toil, our sleepless babies, our children struggling at school, our challenging teenagers, our sick relatives. The image to which he gently but steadily conforms us, if we let him, is no less than the image of his Son.

Assumptions for Sanctity

Both these parents experienced a less-than-easy foundation for their marriage. After her unhappy childhood, Zélie finished school perhaps with a sense of freedom and relief, but money was tight and only allowed for the boy in the family to be educated for a profession. With no funds for a dowry, the two girls, as we know, opted for religious life, but Zélie, forced to reconsider her vocation, realized that her destiny was to marry and have children. But how could she marry within her social class without a dowry? She would have to earn it herself. Zélie thereby built a further foundation for her future: a proficiency in making the "lace of queens and the queen of lace," as it was advertised at the Great Exhibition in London, in 1851.[1] It was remarkable for her time that she became a self-sufficient woman, awarded a silver medal[2] in recognition of her expertise, at only twenty-six. The path Louis chose followed a parallel trajectory toward the goal of self-sufficiency, but having set up his successful watchmaking and jewelry business, he totally supported his wife in maintaining her financial independence through the craft of Alençon lace. As the children came along, Zélie combined a full-time and demanding career not only with motherhood but also with managing her laceworkers, supervising the maids in the household, caring for the older generation, and responding to the needs of family and strangers as the occasion demanded.

It is tempting to assume that, as saints, Louis and Zélie lived such extraordinary lives that no ordinary couple could hope to emulate them. But let's look at this assumption. A man leaves home at five every morning to commute two hours to work and returns after another two hours standing in a packed train to cook his sick wife supper and help his son with his homework. A mother juggles her nursing shifts with child care and just about copes . . . until her two-year-old gets sick and the daycare center won't take her. A trainee doctor, also a mother, a wife, and a daughter, sits up all night catching up on her studies for the next examination. An immigrant works twelve hours a day washing cars in a gloomy parking lot to send his family enough money to feed his children, for whom he aches every night before falling

---

1. The Great Exhibition in London, also known as the Crystal Palace Exhibition, was the first international exhibition of manufactured products.

2. This was awarded in 1858 by La maison Pigache, the first Paris store to sell Alençon lace.

into an exhausted sleep. The list goes on. God is at work. Louis and Zélie demonstrate that it is with this ordinary stuff of quite unremarkable lives that God longs to transform us into the image of his Son.

Dual-Income Family

Couples today often need two incomes to provide for their families, and the church, by raising Zélie and Louis to sanctity as a dual-income family, gives a seal of approval to working couples whose deepest desire is to do God's will within the context of their vocation to marriage. The quandary of work can feel like having to choose between a rock and a hard place. Should one income be reduced or relinquished so one parent can care for the burgeoning family, or is it better to keep two full incomes to give the children what they need now and be in a position to offer financial support in the future? What is "need"? What are the priorities? Can this Normandy couple show us how to walk the tightrope between progressing up the career ladder and focus on being with the children? How did Louis and Zélie keep the balance between work and family? What was it that protected them from the abyss of exhaustion on the one hand and the illusory safety of self-preservation on the other?

Zélie was in fact often exhausted. She paints a picture familiar to many small businesses: "It's this awful Alençon lace that makes life difficult. When I have too many orders, I'm a slave to the worst kind of slavery. When it's not going well and I find myself liable for 20,000 francs out of my own account, and I have to send to other firms the workers who were so hard to find, this gives me reason to worry, as well as nightmares!" (CF 15). A year later, it is no better: "I have a lot of trouble with this wretched Alençon lace which gives me the hardest time. I earn a little

money, that's true, but, my God, it costs me so much! . . . It's
at the price of my life because I believe that it's shortening my
days, and, *if God doesn't protect me in a special way*, it seems to me
that I'll not live long" (CF 20; emphasis added). She felt overwhelmed but, somehow, felt upheld by God at the same time.
This blind faith would help her take a more balanced approach.

Three years further on she was able to advise her young
brother who was setting up his pharmacy business: "I was like
you when I began my Alençon lace business, and I made myself
sick over it. Now, I'm much more reasonable. I worry much less
and resign myself to all the unfortunate events that happen to
me, and may happen to me. I tell myself that *God allows it*, and
then I don't think about it anymore" (CF 26; emphasis added).
We note that after she has *told herself* that God allows it, she does
not worry and waste mental energy on *possible* outcomes, demon-
strating two useful strategies that give us her secret of keeping the
tightrope balance. First, she hands herself over to God's care and
trusts him against all the odds, truly believing that he is protect-
ing her "in a special way." Second, she conserves her energy to
deal with the demands of the day and to plan for the future without being overwhelmed with anxiety about possible disasters and
sinking into helpless depression and despair. Relying less and less
on her own strength, she gradually learned to accept her vulnerability and to relinquish control into God's hands.

Zélie at times loved what she did, preferring it to "nice outings." "To tell you the truth, I only enjoy myself when I'm seated
at my window assembling my Alençon lace" (CF 82). We can
envisage her sitting in a sunny, contemplative space, her fine needle flashing in and out of the exquisite lace patterns and creating something fit for a queen. So often, we too find satisfaction
in the work we are trained to do, but the pressure to achieve

satisfactory and speedy outcomes, the ever-increasing paper-work, and bureaucracy drain our energy.

We can also empathize with Zélie's conflicting motivations to work. Initially her focus was to earn enough money to marry. Later she wanted to give each of her girls a decent dowry, but this became a driving force long after the end was achieved. Zealous to work to the highest possible standard, she lived up to her name. She herself recognized this: "It's not the desire to amass a great fortune that drives me because I have more than I ever wanted.[3] But I think it would be foolish of me to leave this business having five children to provide for. . . . She [Marie, nearly seventeen] curses the Alençon lace and declares she would prefer to live in an attic rather than make her fortune at the same price that I've paid. I don't think she's wrong" (CF 152).

Another aspect came into play: her laceworkers. Toward these humble women, Zélie felt a broader sense of motherhood, a desire to provide for them even when the orders were not com-ing in. She went beyond the bounds of duty, visiting them when they were sick or redoing badly completed work into the small hours, for they had no social security network to help them should they lose their jobs. They, in their turn, were loyal and dependable, so a positive cycle was set up that ensured speedy completion of orders to an excellent standard.

Helping Hands

As the family grew, Zélie needed a hand with the children so she employed a woman named Louise Marais to help in the house. Although described as a maid, Zélie treated Louise as part of

---

3. She and Louis had far exceeded their initial target of saving 20,000 francs for each child as a dowry. See Thierry Hénault-Morel, *Louis et Zélie Martin* (Paris: Les Éditions du Cerf, 2015), 155.

the family: "It's true that I don't treat my servants any differently than my children" (CF 29). Anyone who worked for Zélie went home for family events and national holidays, and their employment was assured if they needed to be off sick. She told her young sister-in-law, "It's not always high wages that assure the loyalty of household help; they need to feel that we love them. We must be friendly towards them and not too formal" (CF 29). She showed this in action later when she wrote, "A month ago my maid came down with rheumatoid arthritis. I took care of her for three weeks. We had to watch over her day and night. I had someone from her village come who stayed two weeks, but she didn't work out. Finally, I had my patient transported [to her home] on a bed by carriage. . . . Since I know she's not going to die from it, I'll wait for her. I'm very fond of her and she of me" (CF 68). Earlier, in her businesslike fashion, she gave not only advice but also practical help to others, as when she found her sister-in-law a cook: "Today I took charge of looking for a cook for you. . . . The capable ones are very sought after and difficult to find" (CF 45). However, broad-minded though she was, Zélie did not tolerate dishonesty and immediately fired a temporary maid for stealing.

Zélie would be the first to admit that she could not have managed without her husband's help. In July 1871, Louis decided to join forces with his wife; he sold his home and watchmaking business in rue Pont Neuf (at a generously low price) to his nephew, Adolph. Zélie's father having died, the Martin family moved into his house half a mile up the road in rue St. Blaise. Zélie ran her business from the ground floor, and the bedrooms occupied the first and second floors. Highly regarded in his profession, it must have been a challenge for Louis to give up his business, but his decision gave him a new outlet—something that was in his blood as an army child: travel. As well as participating in parish pilgrimages, he would now make trips to the grand new department stores in Paris and Lyon with samples of Alençon lace to commission orders for Zélie. These were short breaks from home, but Louis could have become separated from Zélie in the most unexpected and disastrous way, by the Franco-Prussian War. He was willing to enlist as a volunteer but for the time being was too old at forty-seven. The collapsing economy brought loss of income from Louis's shares along with debts from lace orders to the tune of 9,000 francs. With the invasion by the Prussians, the older girls had to be rescued from school in Le Mans, and Zélie was deeply shocked to see the vanquished and wounded French soldiers marching before her window. The family routine was severely disrupted when nine Prussian soldiers were billeted at the house, but fortunately, after only nine days' occupation of Alençon, the armistice was signed and the Prussians withdrew.

WEALTH

Poverty of Spirit

After the war, demand for luxury items increased as the economy recovered. Zélie's reputation for fashionable Alençon lace spread ever wider, bringing in yet more orders. "Now, I'm in absolute slavery due to orders coming in one after the other that don't allow me a moment's rest. I have almost a hundred meters of Alençon lace to make. Last week I received more orders, totaling more than fifteen thousand francs" (CF 78).

Sanctity is often associated with poverty, so it is interesting that both these saints traded in the affluent end of the market. Nostalgia for the Napoleonic era and money from industry created a demand, only temporarily suspended by the war, for luxury goods such as watches, jewelry, and Alençon lace. While Zélie became wealthy through sheer hard work, both she and Louis also received income from significant sums of money in shares from investments and from inherited property. Moreover, Zélie's sister-in-law inherited such a large sum of money from her family that her husband could afford to sell his pharmacy business in Lisieux and devote his life to politics and the church.

Christ himself focused on the challenges facing those who are wealthy when he astonished his disciples by saying, "Truly, I tell you, it will be hard for a rich person to enter the kingdom of heaven. Again I tell you, it is easier for a camel to go through the eye of a needle than for someone who is rich to enter the kingdom of God." In response to their amazement he added, "For mortals it is impossible, but for God all things are possible" (Mt 19:23–24, 26). If we can understand Louis and Zélie's approach to money, we can gain an insight into how God makes holiness possible in all financial circumstances. Let us look at some aspects that evolved during their marriage.

Holiness and Wealth

After long years of training in their respective professions, Louis and Zélie had clear ideas about the use of their earnings: to provide for their children, to help the wider family, and to give to those in need. They invested their money thoughtfully in constructive enterprises, such as the new national railway network.

If they lost money through collapse of the market or unpaid debts, they accepted the situation and simply moved on (see CF 68). Zélie ruefully explained to her brother, "How

I regret not being able to lend you money right now. We're not receiving one cent in income from the Railroad and *Crédit Foncier* stocks. . . . Oh well, what can you do? When this storm has passed, we'll pick up the pieces that are left and find a way to live with less. . . . We receive orders for weddings from all over. There are—and always will be—rich people. It's because of these that, if we are ruined, I hope to still be able to earn my living in the lace business" (CF 66).

Besides lending money as the need arose, Louis and Zélie set aside a percentage of their total earnings for regular donations to charities. Louis recorded this generous amount in the family accounts as "God's portion" (CF 62n159). He and Zélie also responded generously to local disasters, such as floods in Lisieux in 1875.

But charity was not just about money; it was also hands on. If unable to go herself, Zélie would send the maid, Louise, to take money and dishes of stew to the poor people in Alençon, some of whom came to the house and were given food and clothing (CF 159n408). Zélie described one such event: "On our way back [from a walk in the fields] we met a poor old man who had a good face. I sent Thérèse to bring him a few alms. He seemed so touched by this and thanked us so much that I saw he was very unfortunate. I told him to follow us and that I was going to give him some shoes. He came, and we served him a good dinner, he was dying of hunger" (CF 159). Louis later went to much trouble to arrange for this man to enter the hospice, a local lodging for the destitute.

The Martin children learned how to respond to others, not just with money or goods, but also with generosity of time and energy. A vivid example given by Zélie describes the time she met a woman on the train back to Alençon after taking Pauline to boarding school. This woman was traveling more than 600 miles by train (three days and nights) with her two babies to place them with a wet nurse in her family, as she had a job with her husband in southeast France and could not care for them herself. To help her, Zélie took charge of one baby. She teased Louis when he met her at the station and seemed surprised to see her holding "such a badly wrapped package! As he realized I wasn't letting go, he looked more closely and saw a little hand come out. I told him then that I'd found a little girl, and I'd brought her home. He didn't look too happy" (CF 141). They took the baby to the woman's parents' house, and she and Louis didn't get home until midnight.

Work and Family

When running his own business, Louis refused to open his watch and jewelry shop on Sundays, the most lucrative day of the week in secular France. Zélie admired his integrity: "I can't attribute the affluence he enjoys to anything other than a special blessing, the fruit of his faithful observance of Sunday" (CF 140). Other boundaries around work that protected Louis and Zélie from losing a sense of perspective arose from their religious observances, their need for God to be the pivot of each day. As well as daily Mass, they went to fraternity meetings, participated in parish events, and ended each day with family readings and prayer. Somehow, they also fitted in time for family outings, walks in the Normandy fields, and much fun and laughter. Life was not boring in the Martin household!

There was a constant tension between Zélie's need to work and the needs of her family, especially when the children were ill. When Marie was sent home from school with typhoid fever, caring for her was a struggle. Marie wanted only her mother to be with her, and Louis couldn't bear to see his precious "diamond" so ill. "My husband is devastated, and he never leaves the house. He played nurse this morning because, today being Thursday, I had to receive my workers all morning, and he replaced me. But it makes him sick to hear her moan and takes away all his courage" (CF 91). Louis may have felt out of his depth as a nurse, but he played his part in helping when he could. His strength lay in prayer and pilgrimages. Martha and Mary were combined in these parents!

When Zélie's father was ill and she really wanted to be with him, she told her brother,

> I've had enough problems. All of a sudden business has woken up. I received some urgent orders, very urgent. If I don't fill these orders, I'll lose a lot. I'd like to fill them all, and I don't know how to do it. Only a moment ago, I received a letter with an order I have to deliver on the 18th [in ten days]. I don't know which way to turn anymore. I'm up from four-thirty in the morning until eleven o'clock at night. All my time should be for my father, and I shouldn't have anything else on my mind. (CF 33)

Six years later she described her anguish in a heartrending letter to her brother and sister-in-law: "The big merchants in Paris are begging me to make Alençon lace. . . . But how can I want to run a business like this when I have to pull the work out of the workers and take care of my children? It's too much. With all my heart I want this to change and very quickly. I'd prefer to be less rich and have a little rest" (CF 114). In her yearning, she voices a sentiment that certainly rings true for all overstretched parents.

CONCLUSION

We have seen how Zélie and Louis were utterly involved in the events of their day. They speak to us not from theory or theology but from experience. They lived and worked through turbulent politics, war, and the industrial revolution, but they also experienced the daily irritations and blessings, anxieties and joys, of ordinary family life: raising children, earning an income, and caring for the wider family. These aspects of all our lives can feel so mundane that we are tempted to ignore them, to look to the big events as being the moments when God steps into our lives.

Zélie and Louis are relevant to us not because they are paragons of virtue, nor because they demonstrate models of "success," and not even because their faith carried them through the sufferings and sorrows they experienced, but because they embraced all the daily experiences of life with a sense of humor, compassion, and perseverance, all based on a profound trust in God. The tension between the demands of work and family was a source of anxiety and exhaustion but also the stimulus for spontaneity, creative love, and mutual enjoyment. Called to married life, they drank the cup of each day to the full, allowing God to shape them, justify them, and finally glorify them through their work, family, and friends—for richer for poorer, in sickness and in health.

QUESTIONS FOR REFLECTION

- Are there any members of your family set apart by shameful secrets or family feuds? Do you see it as a priority to allow God to heal any bitterness and make a determined effort to be reconciled with them?

- How is your work-life balance? Do you support each other as a couple, or is there conflict? Are there changes you would like to make?

- As a couple, how do you live Christ's injunction to be poor in spirit? How do you share your gifts with others, be it in money, in time, or in joyful spirit?

7

Terminal Illness

When your soul is burdened and fatigued by the weight of your body, do not be discouraged, rather, go by faith and love to Him who said: "Come to me and I will refresh you." As for your spirit, never let yourself be depressed by the thought of your sufferings.

—ST. ELIZABETH OF THE TRINITY (L 229)

FACING ILLNESS AND DEATH

Dying is difficult. It is a venture into the unknown, a journey along a path of mental and physical suffering not only for the person who is dying but also for the family and all those who love their sick husband or wife, father or mother, brother or sister, friend or neighbor. Dying can even feel like a failure, a "giving in" to the illness, a lack of stamina in finding another cure, or a fear of following another course of debilitating treatment. The person's measure of response to treatment is safe to share with others, but the unknown destination, death, is not a subject for discussion. The empty space this leaves in a conversation can make a person who is suffering from a terminal illness feel very alone.

Zélie Martin suffered from breast cancer for twelve years (April 23, 1865, to August 28, 1877) but openly lived with it as a terminal illness for only the last eight months (from December 17, 1876). She is a saint who knows the psychological and physical suffering involved; her husband is a saint who knows the desperation and shock of discovering that the one who is the mainstay of your life is going to die. So then, how can this husband and wife be of help to those who are suffering from a terminal illness today? Can they offer any solace to families and caregivers? The reality of death and of our own dying touches us all eventually, so these people from the past are relevant to everyone who is given some warning of death.

Suffering is Normal

It might be assumed that Zélie *desired* to suffer to get to heaven, as her sister at the convent thought: "She thinks I desire great suffering because I told her, if I had the choice, that I would prefer to die from a slow illness. But great suffering, no. I don't have enough virtue to desire that; I dread it!" (CF 173). It is true that in nineteenth-century Europe people lived with suffering and death as an ever-present reality. Men, women, and children died every day from tuberculosis, typhoid, measles, and other infections; accidents on the roads and accidents in the factories; war; starvation; and natural disasters such as floods. Mothers died in childbirth; infants died of neglect. A person could be of robust health one day, sick the next, and in a coffin on the third day. Commenting on just such a situation in her street, Zélie said, "Every week there are sudden deaths here, and we risk nothing being ready" (CF 175).

Jansenistic Influences

As we have seen, the Jansenistic influence of the time stipulated that salvation had to be "earned" through good works, suffering, and obedience, stirred with a good measure of misery—there was much to be said for living in readiness and not being surprised by death. Worried about the temptations open to her brother in Paris, Zélie wrote, "You well know that life is not long. You and I will soon be at the end, and we'll be very grateful that we lived in a manner that doesn't make our last hour too bitter" (CF 1). This last comment suggests that Zélie believed a good life would earn a good death. As she moved through the phases of her married life and saw her father die and her children born and also die, Zélie told her brother with her wry sense of humor, "As for me, I'm not afraid of going to Purgatory; suffering seems completely natural to me" (CF 42). Eight years later, she wrote to her sister-in-law, "Oh well, we only live to have torments of every kind. . . . If I were alone and had to endure all over again what I've suffered these last twenty-four years, I would prefer to die of hunger, because just the thought of it makes me tremble! I often tell myself that if I had done half of all this [work with Alençon lace] to win Heaven, I could be a canonized saint!" (CF 152).

When death did approach her, however, Zélie showed that her feet were firmly on this earth. Writing seven months before she died, she says, "I'm impatiently waiting for a pilgrimage to Lourdes, and certainly, if my family needs me, I'll be cured, because it's not faith that I'm lacking. Nor do I lack the will to live, the future has appealed to me for some time. My illness may have thrown a little water on the fire, but it's still not completely extinguished" (CF 186). Perhaps Zélie felt ready for death when it was over the horizon, but for her as for everyone, it was more difficult to let go of life as the day crept closer.

THE BEGINNING OF ZÉLIE'S CANCER JOURNEY

Fear

Although Zélie mentioned the shortness of life in warning her brother about the perils of Paris, there was no indication at that stage that she had anything wrong with her. The first warning came two years later, in April 1865, when she wrote to him again, still in Paris where he was studying medicine: "Today I have a gland in my breast that worries me, especially since it started to be a little painful. However, when I touch it, it doesn't hurt, although I feel some numbness several times a day, every day. Well, I don't know what else to say about it, but what's certain is that it's making me suffer" (CF 13).

Questions

In the same letter, Zélie told her brother that she was completely willing to have an operation but that she knew nothing about the surgery. What would it entail? Should she go to Paris, as she did not have confidence in the doctors in Alençon? She was not afraid for herself but was worried about Louis and how he would cope, so she ended her questions with, "Be kind enough to tell me your thoughts on this subject as soon as possible."

There is a sense of urgency here, as if Zélie knew the lump could mean something serious. She attributed its origin to hitting her breast as a young girl on the corner of a table, but the tone of her letter goes beyond a concern about an injury incurred nearly thirty years previously. Her brother was in a good position to arrange for his sister to see the best surgeon in Paris so she could get a diagnosis and make an informed decision. Despite this, however, we hear no more about the "gland" again until October 20, 1876 (CF 168), a full eleven years later.

Isolation

In the meantime, there is no direct information as to what Zélie was suffering physically and mentally from this growing and untreated lump in her breast. She was on her own in the uncertainty. When she felt ill, was it due to cancer, or was it a normal reaction to the stress of her life? Certainly, work made her ill at times, and perhaps she alluded to the growth when she said in December 1866, "If God doesn't protect me in a special way, it seems to me that I'll not live long. I could easily be consoled by that if I didn't have any children to raise. I would greet death with joy, 'like one greets the sweet, pure dawn of a beautiful day'" (CF 20). She seemed already to be thinking about her children, should she die too soon.

Two years on, in November 1868, she said, "Many people believe that I don't have long to live. I hope they're wrong because I don't have time to die; I have too much work at the moment" (CF 42). This was said in the context of her grief for her father and fears that her unborn baby (Céline) would die, but her own death was clearly on her mind. She corroborated this after the trial of finding a third wet nurse for Céline: "I feel I'm wearing myself out, and I have the impression that I won't live long" (CF 48). Perhaps she had a premonition when she said, "We know that life is short, and soon we'll see them [the babies who had died] again. As for me, I'm afraid this will be sooner than I would like, because I've felt very tired for some time" (CF 73). Was the exhaustion due to work or due to the tumor?

Review of Life

In February 1876 when she was telling Pauline that she would like her and Marie to be saints, Zélie added, "I, also, would like to be a saint, but I don't know where to begin. There's so much to do that I limit myself to the desire. I often say during the day, 'My God, how I would like to be a saint!' Then, I don't do the work! Though it's high time I started because I could very well do what two people did this week; they died, and their deaths affected me noticeably" (CF 154). She may have been laughing at herself, but underneath the joking she was deeply shaken by other people's deaths and wondering how she would stand up to the mark when it became her turn to cross the threshold into the next life. What was the "mark" for her? Certainly, it implied even more effort on her part, but there was little reserve energy or time for "doing the work" in her busy days. Was she beginning to realize that the work of making lace and the work of becoming a saint were one and the same?

A Period of Waiting

Until her disclosure of the truth of her condition, Zélie wrote only about her children, local events, and her Alençon lace business; her letters gave nothing away about the growth. Consequently, we do not know whether Zélie sought any other advice at the early stages of her breast lump, but she seemed to have decided against surgery at that stage and saw no need to inform Louis or the children. Aware of God's care for her, she would have placed this issue in his hands, as she told Pauline. "As for me, I know God takes care of me, and I've already noticed it many times in my life. How many memories I have of this that I'll never forget" (CF 156).

Denial

After eleven and a half years, Zélie took the opportunity of a visit from her brother and his wife to update them on her "bothersome gland," after which, on October 20, 1876, she told her sister-in-law,

> As for being unduly distressed over my bothersome gland, I'm not convinced it's necessary. If God allows that I die from it, I'll try to accept it as best I can and resign myself to my fate to lessen my time in Purgatory. But I hope all will be well. I'll make your remedies exactly to put my mind at rest because I don't have great confidence in all that. . . . Please, don't worry about me. In no way am I suffering from the gland, and the little shooting pains I thought I felt are completely gone. I think it will be nothing, or, if it's serious, it will only be much later, when it will be time to die. (CF 168)

Was Zélie now trying hard to persuade herself that there was nothing to worry about, having seen their concern?

After years of apparent denial that the first sign of a lump was anything serious, Zélie now revealed conflicting emotions: optimism and realism, preoccupation with the progress of the tumor, and boredom with talking about the "booboo." She clung to any reduction of symptoms as a sign of remission, as when on New Year's Eve, just two weeks after giving her bad news, she said, "I think I'm cured, or on the road to being cured" (CF 180). Sometimes the pain was severe, but then she would apologize for mentioning it and say it had gone, it was nothing.

THE PIVOTAL POINT—REALITY OF DEATH

Diagnosis

It seems Zélie was more worried than she admitted, for only three months later she took herself to a doctor, as she described in a long letter to her sister-in-law:

> My heart is pounding thinking of how much I'm going to hurt you. I hesitated a moment whether or not to tell you the entire truth, but I feel I must; I need your advice.
>
> I'd made up my mind, last Sunday, to go find a doctor. I was more worried than I wanted to make known, seeing my disease getting worse. If I delayed so long, it was because I was doing my brother's remedy, and he didn't advise me to see a doctor.
>
> I also knew there was nothing to do except have an operation, and the thought of that makes me tremble. Not because of the suffering, but because I was convinced that from that moment on, I would go to bed and never get up again. . . .
>
> My husband, reading your letter, began to become more worried. He went to find Monsieur Vital Romet because I was saying I didn't want to see a doctor. Monsieur Vital came and insisted on an operation, naming several ladies whom I knew and who'd pulled through.
>
> In the end, I went to see Dr. X,[1] who, after having examined me thoroughly through touch, said to me after a moment of silence, "Do you know that what you have there is of a very serious nature? It's a fibrous tumor. Would you

---

1. A doctor in Alençon; his identity is not known.

shrink from an operation?" I answered "No, although I'm certain that instead of saving my life, this operation would shorten my days." I added proof to support this, so much so that he continued immediately, "You know as much as I do, all this is the truth. Also, I can't advise you because it's quite uncertain." (CF 177)

Her brother now tried to persuade her to see a doctor in Paris for a second opinion regarding surgery. But Zélie told him in no uncertain terms, "You put death in my heart with your operations. I know enough about it to be sure that my days would be shortened by it. . . . Don't worry, you'll see that I'm not dying, I'm absolutely fine except for this little booboo with which I can live many years, if they leave me alone" (CF 178).

Surgical Option

In fact, Zélie was between a rock and a hard place. As the need for antiseptic techniques in surgery was not yet accepted, and infectious diseases in hospitals were rife, survival rate of any surgery in a Paris hospital was poor.[2] Zélie would have been offered a radical mastectomy, which included removal of the lymph nodes under the arm. This procedure resulted in swelling and stiffness of the arm, rendering it heavy and clumsy, if not unusable. In addition, removal of the chest muscles caused debilitating weakness of the affected shoulder and arm.[3] In reality, doctors

2. See From our Special Correspondent, "Parisian Medical Intelligence", *The Lancet*, Volume 79, Issue 2004, January 25, 1862, accessed September 26, 2020, *https://www.sciencedirect.com/science/article/pii/S0140673602585603/*.

3. In 1882, seventeen years after the first sign of Zélie's tumor, William Halsted in New York perfected the technique of radical mastectomy with a much higher survival rate.

had nothing to offer except palliative creams and lotions, which Zélie knew were useless. Some doctors may have proceeded with surgery regardless to protect the patient from pain and certain death, but this was "very nearly a practice of euthanasia."[4]

Whether Zélie had any inkling of this or not, if she had survived an operation to remove her tumor in 1865, she would have lost at least some use in one arm, making it difficult if not impossible to continue her delicate needlework with Alençon lace. As Monsieur Vital had told her, she knew women in Alençon who had "pulled through" and would have been aware of the effects of surgery. Clearly their outcome did not win her over, for she decided to stick with Dr. X who was "far from advising me to have an operation" (CF 178). However, she did agree to go to Lisieux over Christmas 1876 to consult with a famous surgeon there, Dr. Notta, who, she said, "finds it very regrettable that, from the very beginning, they didn't do the operation, but now it's too late" (CF 179). By the end of the month, this intrepid woman was saying, "I think I'm cured, or on the road to being cured, because I haven't felt the slightest pain since Thursday. In any case, I'd be able to go a very long time like this" (CF 180). Hope was springing up in her mind.

The Power of the Consultation

In June the following year, Zélie went back to Dr. X to find out if there was anything else that could be done for her. She told her sister-in-law about a most unhelpful consultation:

> He didn't seem to know what I was asking of him. Finally, he wrote me a prescription.

4. Therese Taylor, "Purgatory on Earth," *Social History of Medicine* 11, no. 3 (1998): 391.

Seeing that he'd decided to say very little, I tried to pull a few words out of him. I asked him if he thought the tumor would soon burst, and I got no answer.

I asked him again if he thought they could perform the operation, and he answered, "You well know that idea was abandoned." Then, finally, he said to me, "It's so much better if it does burst, the illness will run its course that way." I answered, "Yes, when I'll die." "Yes that's possible," he admitted, "but it's not impossible that you'll be cured. We don't know how it will turn out."

All of this was said in an indifferent, bored tone with a forced grin that made a profound impression on me. . . .

If I'm not cured, I'll never go back, and he'll never treat me again because just the sight of him would make me sick. Nevertheless, he once did me a favor, it was the day he told me the truth. That consultation was priceless for me. (CF 207)

Zélie appreciated the honesty, information, empathy, and kindness she had received at the first consultation. Now, instead, she was given a prescription for some useless medicine, reticence, dreadful news with a smile (about the tumor bursting), and an utterly false hope of the possibility of a cure. The truth was what she found most useful.

Informing the Family

The effect of informing her family was predictably traumatic. Four-year-old Thérèse clung to her mother even more and developed asthma. Pauline, in her last year at boarding school, suffered constant headaches, and Léonie's relationship with her mother dramatically changed. After years of conflict, this challenging child was freed from the maid's abusive control and wanted to make up for lost time by loving and being as close to her mom as possible.[5] Zélie explained to Pauline, "That is why I feel needed, if not indispensable, so, I very much hope the Blessed Mother will cure me" (CF 201). The children's reactions gave a bittersweet incentive for Zélie to spend more time on earth.

Louis was devastated and inconsolable. He gave up fishing, put his rods in the attic, and lost interest in joining his friends at the Vital Circle.[6] However, like Zélie, after the shock he did not sink into despair but insisted on finding other experts for his wife to consult. He also persuaded her to make a pilgrimage to Lourdes, where Our Lady had appeared to Bernadette at the very time that he and Zélie were married. Surely, she would answer the prayers of all the family for Zélie's cure!

TRANSFORMATION

Held by God

By this stage, any lingering Jansenistic approach to her cancer, such as a desire to suffer to save souls or to appease a vengeful God or even to earn her place in heaven, was subsumed into a complete trust in God. "So, let's put it into the hands of God because He knows much better than we do what we need. It is He who causes the wound, and He who binds it" (CF 179). This was not a sudden revelation but a gradual transformation of her image of God over the duration of her marriage. Initially, she believed God gave people burdens according to their strength (to make them worthy of heaven) as she said, "God only gives

---

5. Louise Marais was emotionally abusing Léonie through fear. An account of this episode will be given in chapter 8.

6. A men's group set up by Vital Romet, a friend of the family, to discuss religious matters, play billiards, and put on entertainments for the young people.

us what we can endure" (CF 6) and, "But God, who is a good Father and who never gives His children more than they can bear, has lightened the burden" (CF 34, 1868).

The next year she could say, "The best thing to do is to put everything in the hands of God and await the outcome in peace and abandonment to His will. That's what I'm going to try very hard to do" (CF 45); and in 1870, "The wisest and simplest thing to do in all this is to resign oneself to the will of God and to prepare oneself to be ready to carry one's cross as courageously as possible" (CF 51). However, old habits cling on, for she also said, regarding people who have too much prosperity, "Never has He led His chosen ones down that road. They have passed through the crucible of suffering beforehand to be purified" (CF 81).

Zélie herself would now pass through this crucible, but the suffering brought not a grim determination to earn her reward but peace. Elizabeth of the Trinity could have been writing to Zélie, as from one dying woman to another, when she said, "In the saddest times, think that the divine artist is using a chisel to make his work more beautiful, and remain at peace beneath the hand that is working on you" (L 249; cf. LF 3.57).[7] God was still Zélie's stonemason, now using a finer chisel.

Resignation

We have seen how Zélie sympathized with her brother, worrying about his new pharmacy business. She said that while she used to lie awake and have nightmares about her business, and indeed continued to worry about little things, "when it's a real

---

7. St. Elizabeth of the Trinity was writing from the Dijon Carmel (196 miles southeast of Paris) in January 1906. She would die, at age twenty-six, from Addison's disease on November 9 in the same year.

misfortune, I'm completely resigned to it and await God's help with confidence" (CF 140). This approach was a preparation for the biggest misfortune, to lose her life, so she would be able to say seventeen months later, "Finally, God is granting me the grace of not being afraid. I'm very calm, and I find myself almost happy. I wouldn't change my lot for anything" (CF 189).

After her experience of mourning for her children and her father, Zélie now mourned for herself. On her deathbed she would say to her children, "Ah! My poor children. I can no longer take you for a walk, although I have been so anxious to make you happy! And I had so desired to give all the pleasure I could to Pauline during her holidays; now I must leave her to herself, or let her go out without me. O dear little ones, if I could only go with you, how happy we should be."[8]

Desire to Be Cured

Zélie had no wish for suffering and, as the growth became more obvious, spoke of her trust in our Lady: "In fact, I don't count on anything anymore except the help of the good Mother! If she wants, she can cure me, she's cured much sicker people. However, I'm not convinced that she'll cure me. After all, this very well may not be the will of God. Then we must resign ourselves, and, I assure you, that is what I'm doing" (CF 181). However, she did not want Pauline to worry and prematurely leave school, so she wrote to tell her optimistically that even if "our good Mother" did not cure her she would live for years.

In February 1877, Zélie described a new lump in her neck. Informed as well as she was, she may have realized that this was a

---

8. Marie Martin, letter 2, to her aunt Céline Guérin, August 9, 1877, in Martin and Martin, *A Call to a Deeper Love*, 369.

spread of the disease, for the spread of cancer into lymph glands was medically recognized by then.

She said of this, "If God wants to cure me, I'll be very happy because, deep down, I want to live. It's hard for me to leave my husband and children" (CF 189). She was more worried about their impending loss than her own death.

One wonders if Zélie was bolstering people up with positive comments about living many more years and even being cured by our Lady, but in her own spirit she was letting go and subtly preparing her family for the possibility of an early death.

LAST DAYS

After her first consultation with Dr. X, Zélie was glad for his frankness "because I'm going to hurry to put my affairs in order so as not to leave my family in an awkward position" (CF 177). Laughing at the thought of all this turmoil making her a saint and far from sinking beneath waves of passive resignation to her fate, she took charge of the situation. She and Louis decided to sell the lace business, but having delayed the sale by honestly alerting the potential buyers to difficulties, she then felt over-whelmed. "Oh well, I'll continue until further notice, and we'll see what we'll do, but I'm very weary of business. I don't have the necessary energy anymore. I feel I need rest, but I'll hardly have any before the eternal rest" (CF 183).

Lourdes

Bowing to her husband's urgent injunction and hoping against hope for a cure, in June 1877, Zélie set about arranging to join a pilgrimage to Lourdes. However, before a possible miracle, she would get her illness certified by Dr. X. She would not take

Louis, as she knew full well how much he loved pilgrimages and would want to visit other holy sites en route. She would travel with Marie and Léonie, stopping over to pick up Pauline from the Visitation convent at Le Mans. The two youngest, Céline and Thérèse, would remain with their father.

The long train journey to the Pyrenees proved disastrous. She found herself caring for the girls, who had sworn they would care for her. Zélie told her sister-in-law, "Sometimes one of them was thirsty, sometimes another one was hungry. What's more, Marie was afflicted by a big speck of dust in her eye and moaned about it for four hours. Finally, Léonie's feet were swollen, and she cried because her shoes were hurting her" (CF 209). The girls were sick from the swaying, lurching train, and the last straw was that another passenger spilled hot coffee from a flask all over their bags, soaking their spare clothes. When they finally pulled into the Lourdes station at five o'clock in the morning, the hotel they had booked was so bad that they had to find another one.

As soon as she arrived at the grotto, Zélie went to the spring. It was daunting. "I looked with terror at the freezing water and the deathly cold marble. But I had to do it, and I courageously threw myself into the water. Yes, but . . . I almost couldn't breathe, and I had to get out almost immediately." Before they left, she described how she again "plunged into the spring four times. The last time was two hours before we left. I was in the icy water just above my shoulders, but it wasn't as cold as the morning" (CF 209). The whole exhausting experience culminated in her slipping on some steps and jarring her neck. The tumor had spread into the vertebrae, which were damaged by the impact and pressed on the nerves in her neck, causing her acute pain. Her own words summarize the experience: "Tell me if one could have a more unfortunate trip?" (CF 209). On the return journey, this indomitable woman sang songs on the train to cheer up the three girls, whose hopes that their mom would be cured were utterly dashed. As a last straw, Zélie was misinformed about the departure time for the first train back to Le Mans so they caught the later train. As a result, a very despondent Pauline had to return to boarding school by herself so the rest of the family could remain on the train to meet Louis at Alençon.

Zélie returned home from Lourdes to a disappointed husband who had been waiting for the "famous telegram" announcing her cure. But her cheerfulness lifted everyone's spirits, and she felt invigorated by a feeling of confidence, still hoping that God would give her a few years to raise her children.

Pain

The pain in her neck after her fall at Lourdes would ease off during the day, and she learned how to support her neck at night so she could sleep. By July 15 (three weeks after their return) she told Pauline it was better, "even a lot better" (CF 214), joking that, as Pauline wanted to suffer for her, to "go right ahead, my Pauline! And for my part, I would have maybe a hundred years in Purgatory to do! Do you want to do that for me too? If you're taking it on, you might as well take it all!" (CF 214). Léonie caught on to this idea and decided that she felt sick and was dying on behalf of her mother, but a few minutes later said she wanted some embroidered slippers. Her mom teased her, "But since you want to die, it would be a waste of money" (CF 214). Throwing Jansenism to the winds, Zélie added joy and laughter where there was sadness and despair. Pauline was due home for the long vacation, and all sorts of family outings to the countryside were planned.

The mood of joy and hope was short lived. On July 24, Zélie twisted her neck again while Marie was combing her hair. They were getting ready for Mass, and Zélie was determined to go, but afterward she swore never to be so foolhardy again while in that state. The effort to walk there and back was excruciating. Now she could not move her neck without atrocious pain and had to try to sleep sitting upright. The slightest movement woke her up. Two days later the pain made her cry out for her brother's help in the night, and she felt "incomprehensively weak," suffering more pain than she had ever felt in her entire life (CF 216).

Terminal Care and Death

The Sisters of Mercy[9] (who had a convent in the town) arrived to take care of her in her final days, and Zélie wrote her last letter to her brother on Thursday, August 16, 1877. "I can't write any longer, my strength is at an end. . . . What can you do? If the Blessed Mother doesn't cure me it's because my time is at an end, and God wants me to rest elsewhere other than on earth" (CF 217). In a letter to her aunt, Marie said, "Papa spent the whole night beside her, he was so distressed. . . . When she is asleep, one would say that she were no longer living; that is the impression it gives."[10]

Zélie died on August 28, aged forty-five years and eight months. Writing now to her uncle, Marie gave a moving account: "Our poor dear father could not restrain his grief. As for our mother, she remained calm and self-possessed. She was to die

---

9. A community of religious sisters devoted to nursing the sick in their homes.

10. Marie Martin, letter 3, to her aunt Céline Guérin, August 25, 1877, in Martin and Martin, *A Call to a Deeper Love*, 370.

thus in a truly saintly way, giving us, to the very end, the example of complete self-forgetfulness and most lively faith."[11]

Throughout the next day, Marie often went to see her body, laid out in a coffin in the house, as was the custom. "I never tired of looking at her. She seemed to be but twenty years old. I thought that she was beautiful. I felt a supernatural impression as I stood beside her. It struck me, which was quite true, that she was not dead, but more alive than ever."[12]

A STORY FOR ALL

Stages of Adjustment

The road of suffering from an incurable illness such as cancer is often dropped into an individual's life as a shock. It feels as if the diagnosis and the information that there is no effective treatment just can't be right—this happens to *other* people. The initial sense of catastrophe and helplessness is then modified as the person moves into the arena of hopes and fears that derive from medical interventions. The person now has a new identity; he or she is a "patient" and enters the world of hospitals, medication, blood tests, indicators of the cancer's progress, relapses, and then new hope, all the while living in an uncertain world where time has a new meaning.

How did Zélie's journey through these stages work for her? We have seen how Zélie responded during five phases of her cancer journey, the pivotal point being the diagnosis. From a long period of uncertainty, the diagnosis moved her into a period of

---

11. Marie Martin, letter 4, to her uncle Isidore Guérin, August 26, 1877, in Martin and Martin, *A Call to a Deeper Love*, 371.

12. *A Call to a Deeper Love*, 372.

transformation, where she adjusted to the reality and handed the future into God's hands. Part of this process involved practical measures, especially the momentous pilgrimage to Lourdes. In blind hope, this feisty lady was determined to do everything she possibly could to be cured. Her last days were filled with unremitting pain, but perhaps in the final moments she did, as she quoted some years earlier, greet death with joy, "like one greets the sweet, pure dawn of a beautiful day" (CF 20).

What aspects of Zélie's journey can work for people today? Her letters reveal nuggets that are of great value for all those who are suffering from a chronic illness.

Family Support

We have seen how shocked and depressed Louis was on hearing the diagnosis and how he urged Zélie to have surgery at the late stage of her illness. He would have wanted progress reports, desperately hoping for signs of remission. His belief in the power of prayer led him to go on penitential pilgrimages for his children when they were ill, so we can be sure that he was praying very much for his sick wife. He was part of her, united with her, so much so that she wrote to him from Lisieux when she went there to see Dr. Notta, expressing her love and her longing to come back home. "I'm rejoicing very much at the thought of seeing you all again. How long the time seems! How I would like to come home today! I'm only happy when I'm with you, my dear Louis" (CF 179). In her husband she found a true friend, a rock of support. We hear little about his role in her illness because he was always there beside her. He knew his wife, her need to be doing things, and perhaps to his dismay she carried on working up to the bitter end.

God's Presence

Against all the odds, chronic illness can bring a person times when there is a profound sense of the presence of God. Christ is with them, in them; he is part of their suffering. We turn to St. Elizabeth of the Trinity, who, from her own experience of unremitting pain, explained, "We see everything in His light, the only true one; and that light shows us that suffering, in whatever form it may take, is the greatest pledge of love God can give His creature. . . . Every soul visited by suffering, therefore, dwells with Him" (L 315). Through the pain, we are changed. Through our vulnerability, we are opened to God's action.

Like Zélie, many people in a similar situation find themselves saying with joy, "It was the best thing that ever happened to me!" This is indeed a miraculous and profound realization that takes away the fear of the unknown. This fear was the natural response to her diagnosis, but the very fear made Zélie turn to God even more and allow him to carry her fear.

Openness

Once her condition was diagnosed, Zélie did not clamp down into herself but was open about how the disease was progressing and its effect on her waking and sleeping. She shared this private part of herself, knowing how important it was to her family, but without any self-pity or unanswerable "why me?" comments. Ever the practical one in the family, she put her life in order as far as she could and carried on making plans for herself and her family. A woman for all times, she anticipated the American Cancer Society's ideas for those who are living with chronic cancer: "Living with uncertainty."[13] People with any chronic

---

13. See "Managing Cancer as a Chronic Illness," American Cancer Society, last updated February 12, 2016, *http://www.cancer.org/treatment/survivorshipduringandaftertreatment/when-cancer-doesnt-go-away/*.

illness often become an expert in their own condition and learn how to manage it. They care for their body through what they eat and how they exercise, and care for their spirit through the support of friends and self-help groups, meditation, prayer, and contemplation.

Little Actions Magnified by God

The experiences of Zélie, her husband, and her children in response to her terminal illness are as relevant to us today as they were at her time of life. Indeed, any visitor to Lourdes will be touched by the spiritual, if not physical, healing that continues to take place in our unbelieving world. When sadness and a sense of helplessness make a family feel useless, when a grieving child feels invisible, when the sick person does not want anyone to know, Louis and Zélie can be a source of compassion and strength.

Zélie spent her working life making and sewing together exquisite pieces of Alençon lace, each pattern unique to the person who made it and the product of hours of work. Similarly, the final lace of our lives is made up of thousands of tiny stitches that join into one magnificent garment, the unique patterns formed from the humdrum events of our days. These "tiny stitches," such as prayer, friendship, and concern for others, are inordinately powerful. Even small signs of care have a profound impact. Hidden and demanding, every one of these little and ordinary efforts is precious to God.

We will let Zélie have the last word: "Then you'll recognize that it's neither your abilities nor your intelligence which you owe your success to, but to God alone. . . . You're going to say that I'm preaching; however, that's not my intention. I think about these things very often, and I'm telling them to you. Now call this a sermon if you want!" (CF 81).

QUESTIONS FOR REFLECTION

- In any life-threatening or long-term illness you or a family member may have experienced or may be experiencing, have you noticed any surprising effects that reflect God's gentle presence in the suffering? How does he give strength in weakness?

- In the event of illness or death in the family, how do you explain it to the children? Does it remain hidden and an out of bounds topic, or can it be an opportunity to take away their fears and help them trust in God's loving care?

- Are you or your spouse suffering physically or mentally? How is that pain affecting you both? Can you both pray for God's grace not to be afraid but to trust that he will bring you closer to him through the experience?

8

The Transforming Experience of Parenting

If I had two wishes, I know what they would be
I'd wish for Roots to cling to, and Wings to set me free;
Roots of inner values, like rings within a tree,
And Wings of independence to seek my destiny.

Roots to hold forever to keep me safe and strong
To let me know you love me, when I've done
   something wrong;
To show me by example, and help me learn to choose
To take those actions every day to win instead of lose.

Just be there when I need you, to tell me it's all right,
To face my fear of falling when I test my wings in flight;
Don't make my life too easy, it's better if I try
And fail and get back up myself, so I can learn to fly.

If I had two wishes, and two were all I had
And they could just be granted, by my Mom and Dad;
I wouldn't ask for money or any store-bought things
The greatest gifts I'd ask for are simply Roots and Wings.

—DENIS WAITLEY

L ouis and Zélie were together for only nineteen years, after
which Louis was a single parent for seventeen years. Zélie's
death therefore provides a natural dividing line between two places
of transformation for them as parents: Alençon and Lisieux.

A MOTHER AND FATHER IN ALENÇON

Zélie joked with her brother that it was not her intention to
preach, but one could say her married life was a sermon. She
ended her days trusting that her death was part of God's plan
for her and her family, but she could not suppress the yearning
to see how she had given the children "roots of inner values"
and the freedom to fly the nest with "wings of independence."
This was her dream but, as she said herself, a dream only to
vanish. Zélie let go of her own dreams and put herself in the
context of all humanity, saying, "My life is not so precious,
and, if I die, there won't be any more unhappiness over me than
for someone else. There are so many people who are dying and
would like to live, who consider themselves useful and whom
God sees fit to take because, after their death, everything will
only go better" (CF 186).

CHILDREN STRENGTHEN THE PARENTS

How could the loss of this mother, this wife, and this vivacious
and deeply loved woman make "everything go better," just as she
was entering the next stage of her marriage? Zélie was deeply
aware of her vocation to bring children into the world, an awareness that Pope St. John Paul II emphasizes in his apostolic letter
Mulieris Dignitatem (On the Dignity and Vocation of Women):
"The moral and spiritual strength of a woman is joined to her

awareness that *God entrusts the human being to her in a special way*" (MD 30).

John Paul does not say that children give a woman credit or honor but that they make her *strong*. They strengthen her vocation. Nothing can prepare a mother for the complete change in her life brought about by the birth of her first baby. All her focus is on nurturing and understanding her newborn, the new human being entrusted to her in such a special way. The first gaze into the eyes of their newborn baby, for both father and mother, has the power to completely capture their hearts in the surprise of love. A lifelong bond is born that perseveres through illness, separation, pain, and disappointment. Challenges such as months of sleep deprivation, or weeks in hospital with a sick child, deepen rather than weaken the bond between parent and child. Forced to change their pre-parental priorities, the vocation of both mother and father is steadily strengthened through their children.

As for all first-time mothers, Zélie wanted to give her children all the love, security, and enjoyment for which she had yearned as a child. Deprived of affection and even dolls to play with as a little girl, Zélie laughed at herself for wanting children whom she could dress up as dolls. She told Pauline, "Nor have I forgotten December 8, 1860, the day I asked our Heavenly Mother to give me a little Pauline. But I can't think of it without laughing because I was exactly like a child asking her mother for a doll, and I went about it the same way" (CF 147).

From Marie down to Thérèse, Zélie delighted in dressing her "dolls" when they were babies. Speaking of her first son Joseph, she wrote, "For his New Year's gift, I dressed him like a prince. . . . My husband said, 'You carry him around like a wooden statue of a saint.' I showed him off, in fact, like a novelty" (CF 21). As the children got older, Zélie ensured they were dressed appropriately for all occasions by taking them on the "endless shopping excursions" that baffled her husband. Through her joy and pleasure in thus treasuring her children, the anguish of Zélie's own sad childhood was washed away. However, clothes were simply an outward sign; she wanted more for her girls.

Zélie wanted the best for her children, and following the piety of the time, the "best" was that they would become holy; the French word is *sainte*, saints. She told Pauline, "I'm going to light my candle to her [the Blessed Mother] as usual, but I won't ask her for any more little daughters. I'm only going to ask her that those she's given me all become saints and that *I may follow them closely*, but they must be much better than I am" (CF 147; emphasis added).

Zélie prayed that her children would become saints for her "to follow closely," not the other way around! The Blessed Mother answered her request in a way she did not expect, for her children strengthened her vocation less when they were a credit to her and brought her "honor," and more when their behavior was difficult and stretched her inner resources. The most transforming aspect of her vocation arose from the pain of helplessness and bewilderment when her previously successful parenting skills had no effect, when a daughter she thought she knew and loved turned into a defiant and miserable teen. That was when Zélie's *strength* was truly bolstered.

Of all her children one was most certainly not cut out to be a saint in Zélie's eyes, because "the poor child is covered in faults like a blanket. We don't know how to handle her, but God is so merciful that I've always had hope, and I still hope" (CF 185). This was Léonie, the one who would make her mother strong, perhaps even make her a saint through her "blanket of faults"! As well as the mother molding her children to be holy and good through her example and parenting skills, of all her children, Léonie in particular would transform Zélie through her exhausting demands and bewildering behavior.

A Challenging Child

Léonie was the "problem child" in the Martin family, physically and emotionally. She had, as her mother described, "continual heart palpitations and an inflammation of the intestines that started when she was born. In short, I saw her hover between life and death for sixteen months" (CF 14). Her little body was covered in eczema, making her itch and scratch herself all over, and her desperate mother could find no cure: neither her brother nor any doctor could offer any treatment that helped this suffering child. Louis took to prayer in a very practical way by walking to Sées (fifteen miles) to pray to our Lady for Léonie to be cured. She recovered her health soon after.

Léonie was late learning to walk, and Zélie described her as "one less beautiful that I love as much as the others, but she won't honor me as much" (CF 13). She was sixteen months when Hélène was born, a baby who, by contrast, enraptured Zélie: "I can't imagine that I have the *honor* of being the mother of such a delightful creature!" (CF 13; emphasis added). But Léonie's new little sister would die five years later, when Léonie was seven.

Unlike her amenable sisters, Léonie was slow to learn, clumsy, stubborn, and prone to emotional outbursts. Zélie was baffled by her behavior, by this child who did not respond to her encouragements or rewards. Louis would step in when necessary, as Zélie described in one episode: "Léonie [age five] is very worried about her little cousin [Marie Guérin in Lisieux]. She made our lives miserable yesterday. All morning long she had it in her head to leave for Lisieux, and she wouldn't stop crying. We had no peace until her father got angry and told her she couldn't go" (CF 29).

We can only guess how Léonie coped with Hélène's death, or how she felt being unable to compete with her brighter older sisters and go to school with them. What was it like for her to be a source of ongoing aggravation to her mother? Perhaps she thought she was only lovable if she behaved, as Zélie illustrated: "Here's Léonie coming downstairs to bring me my rosary, and who's saying to me, 'Do you love me, Mama? I won't disobey you anymore.' Sometimes she has good moments and good resolutions, but they don't last" (CF 169).

Coming into puberty and conscious of her different looks (she had a large chin and more prominent nose than her siblings), Léonie felt so alien from the rest of her family that she "thought that her nurse must have exchanged her for another baby. She confided this fear to her mother, who assured her that she, Léonie, had never been with a nurse!"[1] Pauline felt her sister was very different, as she wrote to her saying, "I shudder when I think of your childhood; you were a cuckoo in the nest."[2] Léonie *was* a Martin child, but why was she the odd one out?

Léonie distressed her mother just by existing, as Zélie disclosed to Pauline: "This child is a great worry to me. When my eyes rest on her, I feel intense pain. She always does what I wouldn't want her to do, and the older she gets the more that

---

1. Marie Baudouin-Croix, *Léonie Martin: A Difficult Life* (Dublin: Veritas, 1993), 23.

2. Jennifer Moorcroft, *Saint Thérèse of Lisieux and Her Sisters* (Leominster, UK: Gracewing, 2014), 59.

makes me suffer" (CF 188). It was not just her behavior that concerned Zélie but her spiritual development. When Léonie was looking forward to being dressed in white again for her second Solemn Communion on May 21, 1876, Zélie bemoaned her lack of spiritual awareness: "Up until now the material side strikes her more than the spiritual. . . . I'm very happy with Marie, and her ideas please me. This is the opposite of Léonie" (CF 159). Marie and Pauline were hard acts to follow.

Hoping against hope that her sister at the Visitation boarding school could have a good influence on her disruptive daughter, Zélie arranged for Léonie to have a trial period there. It was a disastrous attempt, as her sister informed her: "At the moment I am taking care of Léonie, that terrible little girl; she certainly keeps me on my toes. It's a continual battle; she isn't afraid of anyone but me!"[3] After unsuccessful attempts at private tuition, the "terrible little girl" was taught at home by Marie.

Lonely and misunderstood, Léonie was particularly vulnerable. The maid, Louise Marais, found she could control Léonie through fear of punishment if Léonie didn't follow her orders. Zélie noticed the effect on her daughter but not the cause. "I didn't know why she never wanted to take a minute of play-time. When a meal was finished, she would clear the table, put the room in order, and in short, do the servant's work. I was tired of saying to her, 'Go outside and play in the garden. I don't want to see you here while everyone else is enjoying themselves'" (CF 195).

It was perceptive Marie who realized what was going on, as she described: "We had a maid [Louise] who had the unhappy talent of freezing with just a glance my three little sisters, Pauline, Léonie and Hélène; I was the only one she didn't catch in

---

3. Baudouin-Croix, *Léonie Martin*, 19.

her net. . . . I will say that that poor girl made my two little sisters, Léonie and Hélène very unhappy" (CF 195n488). Once she realized how the maid was being psychologically abusive, controlling her daughter through fear, Zélie was horrified: "I would never have believed that one could have done, for so long and so coldly, the things she did to a poor creature who didn't dare complain 'for fear of it getting twice as bad,' as she now admits. . . . I've since learned that the maid had said to her, 'If your mother tells you to go play, go, but you know that afterwards you're going to pay.' You see, all of that outrages me to a point I can't express" (CF 195). The maid claimed to be a great help to Zélie and to be the only one who could "tame" Léonie. But as Zélie noted, "brutality never converted anyone, it only makes slaves of people" (CF 195).

Once released from her abuser's threatening gaze, Léonie completely changed. She would now do anything to be with her mother, as if to condense in the short time available before her mom died all the love and affection she had missed giving and receiving until then. Delighting in the return of her prodigal daughter, Zélie was gentle and nurturing in her turn. She took a page from her sister's book, who had told her that the way to deal with Léonie was through gentleness, not punishment. Zélie was sure that her sister, who had recently died, was guiding her from heaven in how to manage her daughter.

Fears for the Future

Parents with children who struggle to conform will be able to empathize with Zélie when she said of Léonie, "It's her future that worries me the most. I say to myself, 'What will become of her if I'm no longer here?' I don't dare think about it" (CF 184). A few months later, Zélie described how pessimistic she had felt:

"How many times I trembled at the thought of the unhappy future that awaited her" (CF 201).

In summary, Léonie challenged her mother from the day she was born. Despite well-meaning advice from others and unstinting support from her husband, Zélie was on her own as a mother to this child; she took the responsibility on herself. Her sister had written to the Guérins following Léonie's failed attempt at her school, saying, "I saw Zélie, she was quite resigned. She indeed thinks that when our children are not like the others, it's the parents' problem" (CF 117n283). Zélie's final humiliation and sorrow was the realization that her child's impossible behavior was due to abuse by Louise, the maid she had trusted and treated as one of the family. Gradually, her understanding of her vocation to motherhood was refined and strengthened through her child's sufferings and challenging behaviors. Only then was she ready to relinquish her dreams and allow "everything to go better" after her death.

In coping with their wayward daughter, Zélie and Louis were in agreement. They supported each other, refused to pander to her impulsive demands, and instead tolerated her tears and outbursts. While Léonie's behavior elicited frustration and even despair in Zélie, the powerful mother-child bond was revealed not in Zélie's "success" as a parent, nor in Léonie's "being good," but in the pain of the separation they both felt.

Deserving desires for one's children are one thing, but seeing these desires through is another. Zélie and Louis communicated their trust and hope in God's help for them by quiet example and openness more than by preaching and teaching. They both went to Mass every morning and received Holy Communion when permitted, after which Louis would remain silent on the return journey, explaining, "I like to continue my conversation with Our Lord."[4] His friendship with our Lord and integration of prayer into his parenting role spoke to his children without the need for words.

As with Louis, Zélie's first and last resort was prayer. "God is very good to grant me compensations which diminish the bitterness my poor Léonie causes me. I can't get through to her anymore; she only does what she wants and as she wants" (CF 169). She recognized the strength God was giving her in response to this wayward child.

Léonie would not, could not, be fitted into the religious straitjacket of this extremely devout Catholic family. Perhaps she was the lone "free spirit" and in fact the toughest of all the children, given to Louis and Zélie to free them from their preconceptions of perfect parenting. She represents the child who does not live up to parents' expectations, who is unlikely to fulfill their dreams, and who will never satisfy their unachieved desires. While Zélie and Louis carefully watched for and nurtured signs of a "vocation" in their other girls, when Léonie expressed *her* desire to become a Poor Clare, Zélie couldn't take her seriously: "Where did she get these ideas? It certainly wasn't me who put these ideas in her head. I'm even quite convinced that, without a miracle, Leonie would never enter community life" (CF 184). Léonie a nun? She wasn't good enough!

It was only in the last few months of Zélie's life that everything changed. The child opened her heart to her mother, and Zélie opened her heart to her prodigal daughter without recrimination or blame. Zélie's transformation through parenting had reached a conclusion. Her self-image as the good mother who

---

4. Céline Martin, *The Father of the Little Flower*, trans. Michael Collins (Charlotte, N.C.: TAN Books, 2005), 5.

fulfilled her vocation by creating saints had been whittled away. The very depth of her anxiety about her most difficult and suffering child brought her to discover God's action in the most hidden hollows of pain and bewilderment.

Léonie's Sisters

Not only Léonie but also her sisters were instrumental in chiseling their parents into the robust forms they were made to be, parents that would give them roots that were strong and broad.

Marie, at her boarding school in Le Mans, was keen to keep up with the other girls from rich, upper-class families in what she was wearing and the house she lived in. But her mother could see where it would lead her, as she told Pauline: "Here is Marie who dreams of going to live in a beautiful house. . . . Your sister, though so unworldly, is never happy where she is. She aspires to something better. . . . When she has something else, perhaps she'll feel even greater the need for more" (CF 150). Here, Zélie faced the dilemma of how to respond when a child wants to keep up with her wealthier and worldlier classmates. What were the priorities to emphasize? Was there a compromise she and Louis could make?

While Marie and Pauline were thriving, Céline was also an ongoing concern for her mother. "I'm happy with Marie. She usually takes care of Céline, who's learning well. So I won't have to send the little one [age six] to boarding school this year. I would have been quite worried over this because she's a very weak child who needs separate food and eats almost nothing" (CF 144). Louis and Zélie had to adjust their educational aspirations for Céline, considering her age and special needs.

Like Marie, Céline was not immune to false bourgeois values. As a feisty four-year-old, she was once slapped by a poor child. Told to forgive her, she shot back, "Mama, you want me to love the poor people who come to slap me, so that my whole cheek burns? No, no, I won't love them!" But the next morning she had changed her mind and told her mom, "I love poor people very much now!" (CF 105). The slapping episode could have reinforced Céline's discrimination against poor people, but both her parents had already overcome that hurdle, as they exemplified daily, and her mother showed her how to replace her fear and resentment with courage and insight.

How to entertain a bored child? That's a common situation—apparently spanning the centuries—that many parents need to grapple with. When twelve-year-old Marie was still in bed recovering from typhoid fever and missing her sister Pauline, Zélie tried to distract her: "She's bored to death of always being in bed and regrets above all her compositions and the prizes she's going to lose. . . . I try every way possible to lift her spirits. Tuesday evening I made a list of everything she'll do when she's cured" (CF 99). Through her sickness, Marie tore her mother away from her work and stretched her imagination and healing powers to yet another level of patience and responsiveness.

To the younger two girls Marie was a teacher of some authority, as Zélie described in this little anecdote: "Yesterday I wanted to give her [Thérèse] a rose, knowing this would make her happy, but she begged me not to cut it because Marie had forbidden it. She was red with emotion. In spite of this I picked two of them, but she didn't dare go into the house anymore. It was no good telling her that the roses were mine. 'But no,' she said, 'They're Marie's'" (CF 160). In using her rightful authority, Zélie undermined the power she had given to Marie and placed Thérèse in a conflict of dueling loyalties. Even Zélie could not get it right every time!

Through such everyday demands on parenting, the children shaped their mother, and she in her turn left them a legacy they would carry over to the next stage of their lives, in Lisieux.

A SINGLE FATHER IN LISIEUX

At the time of their mother's death, Marie was seventeen, Pauline nearly sixteen, Léonie just fourteen, Céline eight, and Thérèse only four and a half years old. Marie and Pauline were good friends and shared a room on the top floor of the house; Céline and Thérèse were soul mates and shared a bedroom on the middle floor.[5] Léonie, the odd one out, slept alone.

The Move

Before she died, Zélie had looked to her sister-in-law to take over her role as mother to her children. Louis was therefore faced with the decision of whether to stay in Alençon or to uproot the family and move to Lisieux to be near their cousins, the Guérins. He had been advised by well-meaning friends that he was unwise at fifty-four to change his whole life, to leave the place where he had spent the last twenty-seven years, set up his business, been married, baptized his children, and where he would bury his wife by the graves of his three babies and little Hélène. He decided to discuss the options with Marie and Pauline, and perhaps to his surprise, they were not upset at the thought of leaving their home so full of memories but saw the advantage of having a change.

Uncle Isidore found them a beautiful house near his own, with a large garden and close to a park. Named "Les Buissonnets"

---

5. Their room, furnished with a small double bed for the two girls, can be viewed at 36, rue St. Blaise, Alençon.

("The Bushes"), it was spacious and peaceful and gave the bereaved family a secluded space in which to adjust to life without its maternal heart. Louis found a good buyer for the lace business and devoted his time to his family, prayer, and pilgrimages. Marie and Pauline took up the reins of teacher and household manager, helped by a new maid, Victoire Pasquer. The youngest girls found playmates in their cousins, nine-year-old Jeanne and seven-year-old Marie, but Léonie was neither young enough to join her little sisters nor old enough to have a responsible role. She still had not found a niche in the family.

With such a range of children's needs, Louis was facing the ultimate challenge in parenting: how to replace the children's mother and guide them into the adult world. He wanted them to grow strong from the "roots of inner values" that they had set down in their previous life, the roots that had been nourished not in smooth and sterile sand but in "good muck," as a farmer would put it, in the richness and messiness of normal family life.

The Youngest Child

Louis decided to enroll Léonie as a boarder at the Benedictine school in Lisieux, and later, Céline and Thérèse as day students. The challenge to his parenting skills now came from Thérèse, who had lost all her earlier joy and exuberance to become an anxious and tearful five-year-old. She cried at the slightest upset and would not leave the house without her daddy or her sisters. She avoided all strangers and would become ill if left with her cousins without Céline.

Whereas Léonie did find stability and acceptance at school, when the time came for Thérèse to start three years later, it was torture. The shock of the rough-and-tumble of "big" school for this vulnerable and bright eight-year-old who had no experience of playing with children outside the family was immense. She was bullied for being a little know-it-all and teacher's pet, and labeled as having a weak character. In the playground, she wandered around alone or made up her own games. Even at her fond uncle's house she felt she was taken "for a little dunce, good and sweet, and with right judgment, yes, but incapable and clumsy," and she "hardly ever spoke, being very timid" (S 82).

Louis was unaware of his favorite daughter's torment, for she would put her fears aside when safely back home, regale her daddy with her academic successes of the day, and cuddle on his lap while he sang songs and told stories around the fire. When Thérèse was eleven, their father took the older girls with him to celebrate Holy Week in Paris, leaving Thérèse and Céline in the care of their uncle and aunt. However, he was quickly called back when Thérèse became mysteriously ill with trembling and frightening hallucinations. Her beloved father could only stand and look at her, but when "the hat in his hand was suddenly transformed into an indescribably dreadful shape," she showed such great fear that he had to leave the room, sobbing (S 63n56). This sickness caused seven weeks of helpless anguish for Louis, but the source of her recovery was the statue of our Lady in his study. Thérèse recovered her lucidity when she gazed on this statue and saw our Lady smile, her totally dependable Blessed Mother.

Thérèse's illness pulled the family together in a mutually supportive way. Everyone, including the Guérins and Pauline through her letters from the Carmelite convent, worked as a team in the care of the younger children. Louis would entertain the children in the evenings, play games with them in the garden, and take them out, while Marie was Thérèse's guide and caregiver. In fact, Marie so protected her baby sister that she rendered her incapable of looking after herself, as was evident when the eleven-year-old became a boarder for a few days in preparation for her First Communion and shamefacedly had to ask the teacher to comb her long, curly hair.

After Marie had in her turn left to enter Carmel, Louis could no longer repress his concern that Thérèse was being kept as the baby in the family, and unwittingly triggered Thérèse's "Christmas conversion." This came about on Christmas Eve 1886, when the family returned home after Midnight Mass. Although nearly 14, Thérèse had put her shoes by the fireplace to be filled with sweets and little gifts, as was the French custom for much younger children. This year, Louis was irritated with this outgrown ritual and Thérèse overheard him saying to Céline, "Fortunately, this will be the last year" (S 98). Thérèse rushed upstairs, quickly followed by Céline, who, expecting the usual outburst of tears, told Thérèse to wait a while before coming down to open her presents. But Thérèse astonished her sister by immediately coming downstairs with a smile on her face to delight in her slipper gifts, not a tear in sight. As she later described, "I had the happy appearance of a Queen. Having regained his own cheerfulness, Papa was laughing; Céline believed it was all a *dream!* Fortunately, it was a sweet reality; Thérèse had discovered once again the strength of soul which she had lost at the age of four and a half, and she was to preserve it forever!" (S 98). Of this powerful experience, she says, "I received the grace of leaving my childhood, the grace of my complete conversion" (S 98). She found the strength to stand on her own two feet and could now take wings and fly.

Just teenagers themselves, Marie and Pauline allowed Thérèse to remain socially inexperienced and emotionally young for her age, but if they had pushed their little sister beyond her capacity she would have suffered more. Thérèse needed to be taken at her own pace; after so many losses of mother figures, she needed time to learn to trust again.

Captain of the Ship

Louis came into his own after his wife died and blossomed as a delightful but firm father. He was unaware of Thérèse's troubled mind, but he provided her with a haven of security, laughter, and freedom from care. His consistency and peaceful presence were just what the children needed, as a ship provides a haven in a stormy sea. He did not need to understand and analyze all their problems, but he opened their eyes to the beauty of the countryside and God's creation, and he broadened their experience of the wider world so they could make free and informed choices. He shared with them his friendship with our Lord and communicated his contemplative spirit. The teamwork involved not just Louis and the family; God was part of the team also. God gave a fragile and self-centered Thérèse the grace of her "Christmas conversion" when she was ready.

LEARNING FROM TROUBLED CHILDREN

All parents look back on their parenting and say, "If only I had done such and such differently." While recognizing her failures, Zélie did not waste much time in self-recrimination; she trusted in God's mercy and loving safety net and did the best she could at the time. Significantly, it was their oldest daughter who opened Zélie and Louis's eyes to events on more than one occasion, and they were humble enough to listen and then act swiftly and decisively. After the onus of parenting fell on Louis, he too made mistakes and missed major problems in his children's lives, but he did the unstinting best he could. No more can be asked of any parent.

In today's parlance, the children, especially Léonie, pushed their parents out of their comfort zones and were instrumental in teaching them new strategies in response to their troubles. Thérèse brought out immense patience and sensitivity in Marie, who, like her parents, never blamed, scolded, or judged. Marie did not give up; she simply held Thérèse and did what seemed sensible to her at the time.

Small steps cover long distances, and in their small, every-day demands the children drew from their parents deeper and deeper reserves of energy and strength, such as listening at a time it was inconvenient, telling a story when a headache made it the last thing desirable, or letting oneself relax in the fun of childish activities when there is still work clamoring for attention.

For parents who are at their wits end in knowing what to do for a child who opposes their every wish, or another who bursts into tears at every imagined reproof, it is a deep mystery that these "difficult" children are part of God's plan to transform not only the parents but also the whole world. We turn again to the wise words of Pope Francis: "It matters little whether this new life is convenient for you, whether it has features that please you, or whether it fits into your own plans and aspirations. . . . The love of parents is the means by which God our Father shows his own love" (AL 170). This is astonishing! Parents doing simply the best they can out of love for their child, whether they *feel* pleased with the child or with themselves, are channels of God's love. God transforms them through their experience by stretching open their hearts to his unfathomable love.

When their child develops distressing problems, parents often ask themselves, "What did we do wrong?" It follows that, if the Martin parents did everything right, if they have given us a model of perfect parenting, their children must have been well adjusted and happy. The reality was that behind the doors of their bedrooms lived two children who were very unhappy at times. Behind the patina of "perfect parenthood" lay the struggles and mistakes, the misconceptions and sufferings, that make up the common experience of parents today.

It is misleading to think that Louis and Zélie, as pious parents who gave five children to God as nuns, of whom one (so far) is a saint, are a league apart from normal couples. Louis and Zélie started out family life by imparting to their children a model of hard work and rigorous Catholic morality, and ended by living their faith with blind courage and new awareness of God's action in their very ordinary and vulnerable lives. The most difficult child of all, Léonie, was the one who broke the confines of their ideal of perfection.

That they were baffled and misguided parents at times is not the issue. Hindsight is a wonderful thing. What does matter is that they did the best they could for their children in the light of their knowledge and situation at the time. Their example of determination in adversity and faith in a God who *cares* bore fruit in ways beyond their expectations. They were open to the call to growth *through* their children's difficulties, not in spite of them. Normal, messy family life functioned as a path to holiness, as it does today. God is in the messiness.

QUESTIONS FOR REFLECTION

- Do you have a son or daughter who does not live up to your expectations? In your efforts to help your child, who helps you? Do you share your concerns with God in prayer and trust that he will give you the strength and wisdom you need?

- Does the experience of Louis as a widower and single parent resonate with you in any way? What were the key aspects of his life that gave him the strength to not just survive but also flourish as a father?

- As a parent, everything you do with your family is a sharing in God's creativity, love, and gentleness. Can this realization carry you through each day in all the small actions of family life?

9

A Father's Journey

My heart leaps up when I behold
A rainbow in the sky:
So was it when my life began;
So is it now I am a man;
So be it when I shall grow old,
Or let me die!
The Child is father of the Man;
I could wish my days to be
Bound each to each by natural piety.

—WILLIAM WORDSWORTH, "THE RAINBOW"

A MARRIED MAN

Small Things

Louis loved small things. Each day brought delight: a short excerpt from a book that he put in his journal, a field full of flowers that his daughter gathered up, a rainbow in the sky that filled him with wonder. He loved his small children and their little games; he saw himself as small and nothing. He chose a profession that dealt with intricate cogs and wheels, using delicate tools and tiny pieces, that required patience and precision. He assembled minutely engineered bits of metal to make perfect timekeepers and beautiful chimes: watches and clocks that the great and the wealthy were eager to buy.

Every act, however insignificant, was for him with God and in God. His life reflected Joan of Arc's axiom, which became the Martin family's unofficial motto, "Serve God first." In every small event of the day, in every minor decision, in every family gathering, God was actively present: Louis lived not in the hereafter but in the here and now. In the ordinary events of family and business life he lived a balance between action and contemplation. His sensitivity to the importance of life's small events would later become the bedrock for Thérèse's "Little Way."

Some people have accused Louis of being a pious dreamer[1] under the sway of his vivacious wife, a man who lived off his income from his properties and enjoyed the lazy pursuits of fishing or reading by himself. This is a myth. "While he does not have a temperament as active as Zélie, he is not at all idle or apathetic. To the contrary, he is persevering, courageously sticking to the task at hand, meticulous, and endowed with a spirit of initiative, as attested by the success of his professional activity. This will also be proved by his active and capable support for Zélie in her lace business."[2] This married man and widower gives those who discover him a glimpse of how his own vocation as a father is relevant to all fathers for all times. Louis reveals a glorious

---

1. Jean-François Six, *La véritable enfance de Thérèse de Lisieux* (Paris: Éditions du Seuil, 1971), 42. "He is a dreamer and she [Zélie] quickly realizes that it is she who must captain their boat."

2. Clapier, *Louis et Zélie Martin*, 63.

vision of fatherhood hidden in the humdrum reality of family life today.

Quiet Strength of a Husband

In the beginning, Louis was the quiet man in a family of women and children. Household management and family life revolved around Zélie and the laceworkers, while Louis was downstairs with his customers in his watch and jewelry shop. As a self-made woman of independence, Zélie could have lived a professional life in parallel yet separate from her new husband, but she has given us little snippets in her letters that showed how much she relished his love and support. In the fourth year of her marriage, she told her brother, "What a holy man my husband is. I wish the same for all women; that's my wish for them for the New Year" (CF 1).

Many a married woman can relate to Zélie when she wrote to her husband to preempt any fuss: "When you receive this letter, I'll be busy organizing your work-bench for you. Don't get upset, I won't lose a thing, not even an old square, not the end of a spring, in short, nothing. Then it will be tidy from top to bottom! You won't say, 'I only moved the dust' because there won't be any left" (CF 46). One detects that Louis had found himself searching for things she had "tidied away" after previous such dusting and cleaning-up attempts. Their shared sense of humor oiled the wheels of their relationship.

Zélie gave another glimpse into her sometimes-teasing relationship with Louis, when she described a rather mundane event. Telling Pauline about a shopping expedition to buy Marie a complete outfit when she left school, she said, "Oh well, I do nothing but shop every day. Your father says, amusingly, that it's a passion with me! It's no use explaining to him that I have no choice; he finds it hard to believe. But he trusts me; he well knows that I'm not going to ruin him!" (CF 143).

Years later, Zélie revealed her rapport with Louis when she explained to Pauline how she could get her own way with him: "I learned the tricks of the trade a long time ago! So, when I say to someone, 'My husband doesn't want it,' it's that I don't want the thing any more than he does because when I have a good reason, I know how to persuade him of it" (CF 201). In another letter, about her hope that Pauline would continue her studies at boarding school, she told her, "I could well persuade your father. You know that when I want something, little by little I come to get what I want" (CF 214). Sadly, this time Zélie could not get what she wanted as she was to die just six months later.

Although it is Zélie who writes the letters, often she seems to be chatting with her husband or children as she puts pen to paper. Attempting to compose a letter to her brother, she says, "I don't know what else to tell you because I am too distracted. I hear everyone talking at the same time" (CF 11). Frequently working alongside his wife (they each had a desk in the guest room), Louis was ready to include his good wishes to his sister-in-law, "a thousand kind regards" to her brother, or love and affection to his daughter. On one occasion, he gave his compliments to Isidore but told Zélie she should have answered her brother's letter sooner! (CF 11).

They eagerly shared the letters sent in response to Zélie's missives. Louis "laughed with all his heart" on reading a humorous description in a letter from Isidore (CF 12), and he was by Zélie's side when she was afraid to open a letter from the Visitation convent in case it was announcing her sister's death. He gently took it from her and opened it for her. In fact, it was a long letter from her sister just before she died.

Her husband's gentle presence was part of Zélie's existence. Although Louis would go away on business trips and pilgrimages, Zélie herself rarely went anywhere without him. She revealed her strong sense of union with Louis in one of the few letters she had occasion to write to him, when she and the children were in Lisieux visiting her brother: "I'm with you in spirit all day, and I say to myself, 'Now he must be doing such and such a thing.' I'm longing to be near you, my dear Louis. I love you with all my heart, and I feel my affection so much more when you're not here with me. It would be impossible for me to live apart from you" (CF 108). Three years later, she sorely missed her husband when she spent Christmas with her brother in Lisieux to see Dr. Notta about her breast cancer, as the end of her letter to him showed: "How I would like to come home today! I'm only happy when I'm with you, my dear Louis" (CF 179).

Louis rarely needed to write to his wife, but in a letter written early in their life together, he voiced his concern that she was wearing herself out with work, ending his letter with equal warmth:

> I kiss you with all my heart, while waiting for the happiness of being with you again. I hope that Marie and Pauline are being very good!
>   Your husband and true friend, who loves you for life.
> (CF 2-a)

Louis decided to follow through with his concern when he sold his watchmaking business to his nephew, and the Martin family moved over the bridge from rue Pont Neuf to rue St. Blaise.

No extraordinary action emerges from these snippets. Louis simply got on with his job, underwent the common fears and worries felt by many a married man, and supported his wife in all the daily events. The quiet strength of their relationship provided the matrix in which each could freely grow in their vocation.

Contemplation and Action

Louis was notable for his prayer routine and desire for solitary pursuits. Some may see him as a "failed monk," a married recluse who had the leisure and income to follow a monastic routine in the home while his wife earned the money.[3] Indeed, after his rejection by St. Bernard's Monastery and his move to Alençon, he acquired a little tower, the "Pavilion" near his house, where he would go and read and pray in silence, surrounded by his books on spirituality and accompanied by his statue of our Lady that would become known as the Virgin of the Smile.

Aware of his leaning toward contemplation rather than marriage, his mother had feared he would end his days as a bachelor, and it is thanks to her encouragement that marriage and children lifted him from this comfortable groove and set him on a more universal path to holiness. At Les Buissonnets in Lisieux, the "Belvedere" on the top floor replaced the pavilion of Alençon as Louis's place of peace and quiet. The children felt it was a special place for the family, as Céline describes: "With what enthusiasm we annually celebrated Papa's Feastday of St. Louis! We went up to the Belvedere which was decked out for the occasion with flowers and garlands."[4]

The Belvedere was indeed a place of joy on these special occasions, a holy space for reading and contemplation, where Louis's daily prayer nurtured his desire to serve God first. St. Teresa of

---

3. Six, *La véritable enfance*, 43. "The father is more a hermit than a man who assumes his responsibilities as a husband and a father."

4. Martin, *Father of the Little Flower*, 53.

Ávila, writing about spiritual marriage in the seventh mansion of *The Interior Castle*, describes, "All its [the soul's] concern is taken up with how to please Him more and how or where it will show Him the love it bears Him. This is the reason for prayer, my daughters, the purpose of this spiritual marriage: the birth always of good works, good works" (IC 7.4.6). Louis exemplified "good works" born from prayer through his hands-on help for those in need and his designated "God's portion" for charities. In Alençon he belonged to five parish groups. Three involved prayer: the Society of the Most Blessed Sacrament, the Archconfraternity of the Holy Face, and the Nocturnal Eucharistic Adoration; and two groups helped the poor and destitute: the Conference of St. Vincent de Paul and the Catholic Circle, of which he was a founding member. This choice of groups reflected his equal commitment to both prayer and action.

Louis would bear witness to his faith in another active way: by following his beliefs in the face of ridicule from a secular society, sometimes to the inconvenience of his own family. The French bishops stipulated many more fasts, penances, and rituals than we have today, and Zélie would endeavor to invite visitors when her husband was not fasting and abstaining from meat, so they could all share the same meal together and avoid making the guests feel uncomfortable. "You know that Louis is a strict observer of the Precepts of the Church—he would neither want nor eat meat, nor would he not fast for all the riches in the world" (CF 8). Often exempt due to being pregnant, Zélie herself found fasting very difficult.

The church, viewed by the secular society as an institution that took away freedom and fostered superstition, was working hard to reawaken the spirit of the Catholic faith. The bishops encouraged public expressions of faith, such as processions

through the streets on the feast of Corpus Christi, St. Joan of
Arc, and in Alençon, St. Catherine of Alexandria, patroness
of young girls and lace-makers.[5] Pilgrimages were great public events that gave a bold witness to Catholic reawakening. In
May 1872, Louis joined a huge pilgrimage to Chartres cathedral
with 20,000 men, to pray about the religious hostility that was
spreading throughout France. The following year he went to
Lourdes, where his enthusiasm seemed to get the better of him.
Zélie described how he was nearly arrested for breaking off small
stones with a hammer near the Grotto of the Apparition. One
can imagine the flurry of activity, as everyone gathered round
him wanting a piece. A security guard called the police captain,
pointing Louis out as "that tall one there" (CF 109). Fortunately, Louis was not charged and was able to bring two pieces of
holy rock home to his family (CF 109).

Business Matters

Louis took the church seriously and likewise took his marriage vows seriously. He would love his wife, as St. Paul says,
"as his own body" (see Eph 5:28). Seeing her worn down by
work as demand for her lace increased, Louis, who had by this
time sold his own business, put his name to her trade—"M.M.
LOUIS MARTIN, fabricants de point d'Alençon" (Mr. and
Mrs. Louis Martin, makers of *point d'Alençon*)—and took on
the sales and bookkeeping. His business experience and love of
travel made him ideally suited to this new venture. Freed from
his watchmaking enterprise, his artistic expertise quickly lent

---

5. Corpus Christi (the Body of Christ) is a liturgical feast to express Catholic belief in the Real Presence of the Body and Blood of Christ in the Blessed
Sacrament.

itself to his wife's business. He "seized the soul of the lace" and enjoyed choosing templates and designing new lace patterns, even creating the patterns himself, stitch by stitch, in his free time.[6] The intricacy of the *point d'Alençon* was not dissimilar from the fine art of watchmaking: tiny stitches created superb flounces of lace. He would drum up business from the grand department stores in Paris, but he was not a soft touch. Céline tells us, "So also he was very severe in regard to any sign of negligence or carelessness."[7]

A shrewd investor, Louis seemed to have an instinct for the financial market and would not be pushed to follow a questionable deal, even if urged by his lawyer. Only his wife could persuade him to sell any shares at a loss. Céline remembered her father telling her, "I feel that I could easily acquire a taste for investing, but I do not want to be carried away by the current. It is such a dangerous incline, and leads to speculating."[8] Louis thereby avoided the insidious slavery of attachment to money. When France was experiencing a recession, he would joke with his children, "This is what we'll do when we are bankrupt!"[9] He often quoted from *The Imitation of Christ*, "Man's happiness consists, not in having an abundance of material goods, but a moderate proportion that is sufficient for him."[10] Having enough for his family was all he wanted; anything more than that was a bonus from the good God and would be used wisely and generously.

---

6. Hénault-Morel, *Louis et Zélie Martin*, 156.

7. Martin, *Father of the Little Flower*, 31.

8. Martin, 31.

9. Martin, 32.

10. Thomas à Kempis, *Imitation of Christ* (New York: Alba House, 1995), 1.22.

After his wife died and he had settled his daughters in Lisieux, Louis remained in Alençon to complete the remaining orders but was impatient to join his children, writing, "I can't wait to be with you again, and I'm urging the workers to finish the Alençon lace that I still have with several assemblers" (CF 218). He then found a good buyer for the business and was free to make the transition to Lisieux and to the next stage of his life.

A SINGLE FATHER

The next stage for Louis was life without Zélie. Her death left a huge hole in his heart and a burden of responsibility on his shoulders. But he felt that Zélie was with him, for in 1885, eight years after she had died, he told his daughters that "the thought of your mother also follows me constantly" (CF 228). By this stage, the memory of his wife brought no longer anguish but peace, for in the same year he told his friend Mr. Nogrix, "I'm living on almost nothing but my memories. The memories of my whole life are so pleasant that in spite of the ordeals I've been through, there are moments when my heart overflows with joy" (CF 220). Through his total trust that all things were in God's hands, Louis had no regrets and no bitterness, however deeply he felt the loss of a retirement that he and Zélie had planned to enjoy together. She was still beside him, helping him to be a mother as well as a father to his children.

His gentle sister-in-law, who had been such a close friend of Zélie, would also be a mother to his children, and his brother-in-law was ready to take his share of the responsibility. Isidore Guérin had a strong personality, but perhaps Céline underestimated her father when she said, "With his outspoken ways my uncle, M. Guérin, rather frightened my father, who was by nature so simple and reserved."[11] All the girls loved and revered their father and were very protective of him, but he was made of equally sound stuff as his brother-in-law.

Isidore had some legal responsibility under the French law of inheritance, for the Civil Code placed the legacy to the surviving spouse second to that of the children and the deceased spouse's family. Regarding major decisions, the children were obliged to gain permission from their uncle, such as when Thérèse wanted to enter Carmel at fifteen. Louis readily accepted and respected his brother-in-law's role and prompted the girls to listen to the advice of their uncle and aunt and treat them as part of the family.

Home and Hearth

Pauline had just finished boarding school when the bereaved family moved to Les Buissonnets, and for the first time, all five girls were at home together. Louis bloomed as the life and soul of his family. Perhaps the child indeed became "father of the Man" as Wordsworth says, for Louis relived his childhood through his children. As Céline tells us, "He used to repeat with a note of satisfaction and pride: 'I am the *bobillon* with my children.'"[12]

The evenings were a time of great fun, for he was a brilliant mimic, storyteller, and singer. He could imitate the whistles and songs of birds and speak in the regional dialects, having come across many provincial accents as an army child. He would read to his children from his favorite books or recite long tracts from

---

11. Martin, *Father of the Little Flower*, 42.

12. Martin, *Father of the Little Flower*, 55. *Bobillon* was a familiar name given to someone tender and kindly.

memory, introducing them to classic French authors such as Lamartine, Chateaubriand, and Victor Hugo. But above all, they were mesmerized by his beautiful voice. His fingers would tap out the drumbeat of military marches, and his sonorous singing would bring to life hymns and folk songs.

One song particularly appealed to young Thérèse, for she would follow the actions by lining up her little wooden figures made by her father, knock them down, and then make them bounce back to life. The ballad is about a short little man called Guilleri who climbs a tree to get a better view during a partridge hunt, but the branch breaks and down he falls, breaking his leg and dislocating his arm. Happily, nurses from the hospital hear his cries and rush out to bind up his wounds, so he survives. The rhythm goes with the words, "*tom*bi, Carabi, *tit*i Carabi, *tot*o Carabi, will you be left to die?" Louis told his children that in the struggles and shocks of life, they must copy "Tombi Carabi" and get up after every fall and always look up above.

We can hear Louis pounding out the song with the girls joining in on the chorus; we can watch Thérèse on the floor lining up her little figures, swiping them down, and then up they leap! The evening draws on, and Louis picks up his "little queen" and rocks her to sleep on his lap, singing a gentle lullaby. The roast chestnuts have been eaten, the logs are flickering in the fireplace, and all the worries of the day are in the shadows.

The evening would end with a prayer the family loved to say together, a prayer composed by a military general known for his heroic action in the Prussian war.[13] The first six lines are as follows:

---

13. General Gaston de Sonis (1825–1887).

My God, here I am, before You poor, small, naked
   of everything.

I am there, at Your feet, plunged in my nothingness.

I would like to have something to offer You,

but I am nothing but misery.

You, You are my All, You are my richness.

My God, I thank You that You want me to be nothing
   before You.

I love my humiliation, my nothingness.[14]

The Child Is Father of the Man

In addition to making figures from alder wood for Thérèse to
play with, Louis was deft at making little working toys such as
carts from melon rind and an ingenious little spinning wheel to
wind off the silk threads from the cocoons of silkworms kept by
Céline. The family also kept chickens, rabbits, and birds in an
aviary, and Tom, the English springer spaniel that Louis gave
Thérèse, no doubt eagerly joined in their garden games. Their
father even taught a tame magpie to speak, and it would provide
great entertainment by following them round the garden and
pecking at their clothes.

Each child had a plot in the yard for growing her own flowers and vegetables, and Louis would send them off on treasure
trails to find surprises hidden in the nooks and crannies, telling
them when they were hot (getting close) and when they were
cold. He would pause his digging to taste their "cups of tea"
and delicious "delicacies" they concocted from stones and fruits
around the garden.

---

14. Clapier, *Louis et Zélie Martin*, 250.

Louis loved the great outdoors and might have been a monk high up in the Alps if he had been taught Latin as a schoolboy. He took the children on walks in the undulating Normandy fields, visiting the churches and fishing in lakes amidst the abundant wildflowers that flourished in the farmland. A true Normandy man, Louis garnered apples and made his own cider for the cellar, and perhaps enjoyed the occasional warming sip of Calvados, the local apple brandy.

Always close to their Guérin cousins, the two families got together every Thursday and Sunday and enjoyed trips to the coast and the countryside. Occasionally, Louis and the girls returned to Alençon to see friends and visit Zélie's grave. During August, the Guérins rented a house by the sea, where the Martins could go at any time, and in September, Louis and the girls would go on the five-mile trip by wagon to visit their great-aunt and spend the day collecting hazelnuts.

Louis was a father whose personality flourished and bore fruit in the flow of family life. However, all was not fun and games, for he "liked order, and carried it out himself very strictly. When something was broken through negligence, he showed his disapproval rather severely."[15] Son of an army officer, he liked to know what was happening and where things were, but he trusted Marie and Pauline to run the household and never interfered or criticized their efforts.

The Wider World

Contrary to an image of living an enclosed semi-convent life at Les Buissonnets, after their mother died the Martin girls had a rich and varied existence. Less than a year after their mother's

---

15. Martin, *Father of the Little Flower*, 50.

death, Louis took the older two girls (ages eighteen and sixteen) to visit the 1878 Paris World Fair. They were so enthu-
siastic about all the sights that they stayed on in Paris for a
second week to fit in the Théâtre français and opera. Besides
the excitement of seeing the first phonograph and telephone in
the exhibition, the sight of Opera Avenue lit up by the newfan-
gled electric lamps mesmerized them. "We all arrived yesterday
in good health, I cannot tell you how excited we were to see for
the first time this huge city of Paris," wrote Pauline to her aunt
and uncle, listing a stream of places they had visited from the
day they arrived.[16]

The whole excursion was an opportunity for Louis to edu-
cate them and open their minds to the wider world, including
other Christian traditions (He took the girls to vespers at a
Protestant church, an unusually progressive step for a Catholic of that era). But after Paris, there was more to come. Louis
wanted to see the wider world, and in 1885 he joined a pilgrimage tour of central Europe and Turkey that lasted almost
two months. Thanks to this separation from his girls we have
an insight into his affection for them through his evocative
letters from stages of the journey, when he addressed them by
their affectionate nicknames. These are given to us by Céline:
"Marie was 'the diamond,' sometimes 'the gypsy' on account
of her independent spirit. Pauline was 'the fine pearl,' then
came 'good-hearted Léonie.' As for Thérèse, she was in turn
'the Little Queen of France and Navarre,'[17] the 'Orphan of the

---

16. Hénault-Morel, *Louis et Zélie Martin*, 221.

17. The queen of Navarre, 1492–1549, was well educated, courageous,
and independently minded. She wrote many plays and poems, and called herself
"prime minister of the poor." The king of Navarre set up a public works system
and education for needy students.

Louis's parents, Pierre-François Martin and Marie-Anne-Fanie Boureau

Zélie's father,
Isidore Guérin (Sr.)

Zélie, Isidore, and Marie-Louise Guérin

Louis Martin at about the age of 40

Isidore, Zélie's brother, as a young man

MH

MJJ MJL

Souvenir du court exil de nos
chers Petits Anges
et de leur Naissance au Ciel

Marie Hélène _ 13 Octobre 1864 _ 22 Février 1870
Marie Joseph Louis _ 20 Sept. 1866 _ 14 Février 1867
Marie Joseph Jean Baptiste _ 19 X.bre 1867 _ 15 Août 1868
Marie Mélanie Thérèse _ 16 Août 1870 _ 8 Octobre 1870

Louis and Zélie's children
in heaven

Zélie with Joseph-Louis
(painted on her photo)

Céline

Pauline and Marie

Hélène Martin, who died
at the age of 5

Thérèse

Rose Taillé

Zélie Martin a few years
before she died

Céline and Thérèse

Zélie's brother and sister-in-law with Marie Guérin, Céline, and Léonie

Marie

Léonie

Pauline

Pauline

Céline and Léonie

Céline and Tom

Léonie, Céline, and Marie Guérin at La Musse

Louis with Céline and Léonie

Berezina,'[18] the 'little blond May-beetle,' or the 'Bouquet.'"[19] He was her "papa king." Céline's nickname was "my courageous one" or "the intrepid." These are fine names for children to live up to! Addressing a letter from the Black Sea to his "big girl," his "diamond" (Marie), Louis ended it with, "Give a big hug from me to my little 'pearl,' as well as Léonie, Céline, 'my courageous one,' and the Queen of my heart. . . . Tell my little 'Paulin' [in the Lisieux Carmel] that her memory is very present to me and that I'd like to send her all the big fish I see from our deck jumping about in the Black Sea. How many there would be heading toward the Carmelite Monastery in Lisieux!" (CF 224).

Son of a Soldier

Born of military stock, Louis not only enjoyed seeing the world but also had a reputation for bravery and courage. He was a strong swimmer, and while studying in Paris, on more than one occasion he rescued a person who had fallen into the river. He was quick to respond in an emergency and had saved a house opposite Les Buissonnets from being destroyed when he spotted a fire and quickly doused the flames.

Louis exemplified this courage many years previously, in January 1871, when the Prussians were marching toward Paris and Alençon was placed in a state of defense. Louis had a wife and four children to protect, aged from under two to nearly eleven years old (Thérèse had not yet been born). Itching to do something to protect his country, he was ready to enroll as a volunteer at age forty-seven but was, for the time being, over the age limit.

---

18. The Battle of Berezina took place in 1812, when Napoleon's army was retreating from his invasion of Russia.

19. Martin, *Father of the Little Flower*, 43.

"My husband is not worried about this at all. He would not ask for any preferential treatment and often says that, if he were free, he would join the *franc-tireurs*" (CF 62).[20]

The Prussians marched into Alençon after shells had hit the town and set fire to the timber-framed houses, forcing families to retreat down to their cellars. Nine soldiers were billeted with the Martins. Unable to take up arms himself, Louis was devastated, as Zélie told her sister-in-law: "My husband is sad. He can neither eat nor sleep. I believe he's going to get sick" (CF 64). But when a soldier tried to steal a watch from his shop, Louis was quick to throw him off the premises and complain to the military authorities. However, learning that the unfortunate man was to be shot as an example, Louis then made an appeal that his life be spared.[21] Fortunately, the Prussians withdrew from Alençon after only nine days, when the Franco-Prussian Armistice was signed on January 28, 1871.

Decisive in a crisis, Louis was equally resolute when it came to the family. When Zélie was agonizing about a child who was being used as a slave by a pair of fake "nuns" whom she had hired to teach Léonie, Louis took her to the police station to file a written report (CF 128). He would also step in for strangers in need, as when he took care of the final expenses and burial for a poor woman who had died but had no relatives or friends to take on this responsibility. Indeed, numerous occasions mentioned by Zélie and others illustrate how he was ready to walk that extra mile for strangers and friends alike.

---

20. The *franc-tireurs* were bands of armed French civilians who monitored the movement of the enemy.

21. For more of this story, see Paulinus Redmond, *Louis and Zélie Martin: The Seed and the Root of the Little Flower* (London: Quiller, 1995), 86.

MISSION ACCOMPLISHED

Wings that Fly

Louis's heart was in his home, but he would not restrain his brood from flying the nest. The first to go was Pauline, five years after Zélie died. Closest to Zélie of all the children, Pauline had her mother's strength and determination and was convinced from her teenage years that she wanted to join a religious order. It was assumed she would go back to the Visitation Convent in Le Mans, where she went to school, but she surprised everyone when she felt called to join the Carmelites in Lisieux. Her father was worried that the life might be too austere for her, so he made sure she had a good diet by bringing the Carmelite monastery a constant supply of fresh fish.

The second to take wing was Marie, who, during a retreat, also felt called to join the Carmelites, a decision that again surprised both her father and her uncle. She was a spirited and independent young woman and had never shown any inclination for religious life. Louis was very sad to lose her. Céline movingly describes his response to Marie's revelation: "Ah! Ah! but without you . . ." He overcame his emotion, embraced her, and then said, "I thought that you would never leave me!"[22] He had assumed that Marie would remain at home to run the household and care for her younger siblings.

Regarding his third daughter, Louis was a calm rock of strength for Léonie during her four attempts to enter religious life. Twice, she left home without so much as a goodbye, which embarrassed Louis and greatly upset Céline. But her father excused Léonie's impulsive decision each time and let events

---

22. Martin, *Father of the Little Flower*, 61.

take their course. When she sadly returned home after just eight weeks with the Poor Clares and after six months (July 16, 1887, to January 6, 1888) in the Visitation convent, her father never said, "I told you so" but was sympathetic and continued to support her as she persevered in her search.

The fourth flight from home and hardest for her father to bear was that of Thérèse, who was just fifteen, and his favorite. Her leaving would break his heart, however much he wanted to accept the loss as a sacrifice to God. To his friends, the Nogrix family, he wrote, "Thérèse, my little Queen, entered Carmel yesterday! God alone could demand such a sacrifice, but He's helping me so powerfully that through my tears, my heart abounds with joy" (CF 230). It was a long quest for his queen and, once he had his hand to the plow, nothing would stop him helping her enter Carmel's door. She was initially refused permission by her uncle, by the bishop, and by the Carmelite provincial. Her father went with her to the bishop of Bayeux, wrote letters, and contacted prelates who could pull strings, but all to no avail.

Louis was glad then to distract his disappointed daughter and take her and Céline on a pilgrimage to Rome, from November 4 to December 2, 1887. "The special train would convey one hundred and eighty-seven travelers, including a certain number of clergy; for the most part, the lay folk would belong to the Norman aristocracy."[23] Céline, in her personal recollections of her father, is at pains to point out that this trip was booked well before Thérèse's request to enter Carmel was refused and was not for the express purpose of seeking permission from the pope.[24] This was to be Louis's last expedition, and he greatly

23. Piat, *Story of a Family*, 351.
24. Martin, *Father of the Little Flower*, 66.

enjoyed showing the girls all the sights, sharing their delight, and no doubt regaling them with historical facts and figures.

CAN ONE BE TOO HAPPY?

The pilgrimage to Rome was Louis's swan song, for his health was failing. The following May, he visited his old parish church in Alençon, where he and Zélie were married and the children baptized. In prayer, he was overwhelmed with consolation and received what he felt was a special grace. He found himself praying, "My God, it is too much! I am too happy; it is not possible to go to Heaven this way. I wish to suffer something for you, and I offer myself."[25] Louis's prayer was to be answered. He had already suffered a small stroke five months previously, from which he had made a good recovery. Two more were to follow, which would have a more devastating effect. This active man who had always been in charge of his life, who was revered by his daughters and esteemed by his friends, whose fine brain brought entertainment and knowledge to others, and whose compassion found its home in so many hearts would make the sacrifice he had requested: he would lose his most important possession, his mind.

With his last letter to his Carmelite daughters, Louis encapsulated his life's achievement: "I want to tell you, my dear children, that I have the urgent desire to thank God and to make you thank God because I feel that our family, though very humble, has the honor of being among the privileged of our adorable Creator" (CF 231).

---

25. Redmond, *Louis and Zélie Martin*, 249.

QUESTIONS FOR REFLECTION

- How do you balance action and contemplation? Could they be integrated to bring God's presence into ordinary activities at home and at work, with time for prayer as the foundation for the busyness of the day?

- If you are or have been a single parent, or know someone who is, what strengths and hidden resources have emerged as a result? How have the children contributed to this creative force?

- Are your Christian beliefs hidden or open? Are they reserved for Sundays, or are they a joyful part of daily family life?

10

Loss of the Mind

To come to enjoy what you have not
You must go by a way in which you enjoy not.
To come to the knowledge you have not
You must go by a way in which you know not.
To come to the possession you have not
You must go by a way in which you possess not.
To come to be what you are not
You must go by a way in which you are not.

—St. John of the Cross, description in "Sketch of Mount Carmel," in *The Ascent of Mount Carmel*

A WAY IN WHICH YOU POSSESS NOT

Dementia

When we reach a certain age, many of us think of the future and worry about dementia in ourselves or in members of our family. Is that increasing forgetfulness a first sign? Perhaps red wine will protect us, or playing the piano, or learning a new language. We worry about how the cost will be covered for a nursing facility for ourselves or our parents. We know about other heroic people but wonder how *we* could cope with being a caregiver of a wife, a husband, a parent. Who would help us? Dementia brings uncertainty and difficult decisions; it brings anguish and heartbreak, and now Louis and the Martin family would have to face these difficulties.

Louis and Zélie Martin are exceptional saints. They touch us because their life experiences ring true for us today: bereavement, sickness, work, war, school, cancer. Their story is the story of all parents, a path through the thicket of dependent infancy, childhood challenges, school successes and failures, growth to young adulthood, and taking wing to the wide world. Their exemplary example as a married couple would be enough to sanctify them.

However, Louis desired more, he wanted to offer God his very being. God took him at his word, and Louis set out on the final stage of his life, a journey into losing his mental faculties. We know he had recovered from a small stroke before the grand tour to Rome with Thérèse and Céline. This turned out to be the first sign of vascular dementia, caused by tiny blood clots progressively blocking the blood vessels to the brain. His response to this disease would give an insight into how this most shameful and bewildering experience of losing one's reason can be a path to holiness for sufferers and their families alike.

The Prelude

Through the relentless progress of his dementia, Louis takes us into the realm of shame and unknowing, the way of dispossession: the loss of his physical strength and the loss of his mind. The story starts near the end of 1875, a year before Zélie was diagnosed with inoperable breast cancer. Louis was enjoying his favorite pastime, fishing by the river. Suddenly stung behind his left ear by a poisonous fly, he thought nothing of it, but the sting developed into a painful rash that motivated him to consult several doctors. The rash was diagnosed as an epithelioma for which Louis was treated with a range of painful but ineffective remedies. After the last series of treatments in 1888, he was in such pain that he could only stride around the garden saying to his children, "I am losing my head! Oh! Children, pray for me!"[1] The rash gradually subsided but continued to cause discomfort for the rest of his life.

On May 1, 1887, ten years after Zélie died, Louis awoke with marked weakness of his left side and distorted speech. Determined as he was, he still went to Mass that morning to receive Communion on the first day of Mary's month of May, dragging his leg along the pavement. He told his girls, "My poor children, we are as fragile as blossoms on the trees in springtime; in the evening we, like them, seem wonderful; the following morning, an hour's frost withers and shrivels us up."[2] As soon as Isidore, his pharmacist brother-in-law, found out, he made Louis go to bed and applied a dozen leeches. Perhaps the leeches worked their wonder, for Louis made a good recovery and was fit enough to take Céline and Thérèse on their memorable trip to Rome in November the same year.

The following January, Thérèse was given permission to enter Carmel, and her farewell party at Les Buissonnets took place in April 1888. After this rather sad celebration, one that was mixed with joy and sorrow for Louis, "one of his friends said to him, 'Abraham has no lesson to teach you; like him, if God had demanded it, you would have sacrificed to Him your little

1. Hénault-Morel, *Louis et Zélie Martin*, 237.
2. Martin, *Father of the Little Flower*, 83.

Queen.' He replied instantly: 'Yes, but I confess, I would have raised my arm slowly, hoping to see the angel and the ram.'"[3]

The year 1888 was one of change. The following month Louis made his total offering to God at his old church in Alençon, and in June, he was so impressed by a painting of Our Lady of Sorrows which Céline had done that he told her she should have art lessons in Paris. But Céline then disclosed a different project she had in mind, life as a Carmelite. He was delighted, as she described: "At this unexpected revelation, my dear father wept with joy, and exclaimed with rapture: 'Come, Céline, let us go together before the Blessed Sacrament to thank the Lord for all the graces He has granted our family, and for the honor He has done me in choosing spouses in my home.'"[4]

A Changing Man

It was not long after Céline's revelation of her call to Carmel that Louis began to show increasing signs of distraction and forgetfulness, had mood swings, and was filled with anxiety about threats of religious persecution by the government. He feared for the safety of his four daughters (Léonie, Pauline, Marie, and Thérèse) in their religious orders and he even prepared a hiding place for priests at Les Buissonnets.[5] He also made uncharacteristic financial decisions by investing unwisely and selling his properties, and when he knew his daughters were safe, he developed a fixed idea that he should put all his affairs in order and retire in solitude to be a hermit. To this end, he would occasionally take himself off to Paris, but to Céline and Léonie's alarm,

---

3. Martin, 73.

4. Martin, 75.

5. See Clapier, *Louis et Zélie Martin*, 274.

there would be no sign of their usually reliable and punctual father on the planned day of return. Waiting anxiously, it crossed their minds that he might have been killed, for he often carried large amounts of money on his visits to the capital. In addition to these planned trips, he frequently left the house without telling anyone, replying to Céline when she asked him why he went, "Yes, I had a goal, it was to love God with all my heart."[6]

These disappearances culminated later that same June, when Louis vanished for four days and the family could not find him anywhere in Lisieux. He was only discovered after Céline received two letters from her father, from Le Havre, the first asking for money and the second asking for the return of the keys of Les Buissonnets. Hurrying to Le Havre, thirty-six miles north of Lisieux, Céline, Isidore, and a friend searched the large port fruitlessly but eventually found Louis waiting by the post office for his money. They were shocked at his state, for he had shaved off his beard to avoid being recognized and had spent the previous three days mingling among the fisherman on the shore. He came home peacefully, where Léonie was very relieved to see him back safely. Alone at home while the others traveled to Le Havre, she had had the alarming experience of seeing the small house next door gutted by fire the previous morning. The wooden edge of the roof of Les Buissonnets had also started burning, but fortunately the firefighters managed to prevent the flames from spreading. Their own home had survived, but the sight of the blackened beams next door did not help Louis's disturbed frame of mind.

Forgetful though he was in some things, Louis remained determined in other ways. He now insisted that Céline should

6. Clapier, 277.

study art as he had promised earlier, and he even rented a chalet for her in Paris. Against all sensible advice but to pacify her father, Céline took Léonie with her to Paris on July 1. Inevitably, with no art materials in the chalet and ongoing concern about their father, they came back after only two weeks. Céline wrote to Thérèse, "Yesterday evening, I felt my heart would break, I mean about this poor little father. He now seems so old, so worn. My heart is torn apart; I imagine that he will die soon, oh! If he did, I think I myself would die of grief."[7]

Céline's presentiment was near the truth, for while visiting Alençon with Céline and Léonie three weeks later, Louis decided to go on to Honfleur, on the coast, to pray at the sanctuary of Our Lady of Grace. Here he had another stroke on August 12, this time a major one. Céline wrote, "Dear little sisters, my pain is so anguished that on walking by the quay, I looked with longing into the depths of the water. Ah! If I had no faith, I would be capable of anything."[8] While "good-hearted Léonie" was a caring and loyal companion, Céline was probably carrying the brunt of responsibility for her father. Did she also feel she had been left to carry the burden by her three sisters in their Carmelite monastery? Although Céline also had a vocation to Carmel, she was the one who had to wait.

The day of Thérèse's clothing, when she would receive the Carmelite habit, approached, but due to her father's poor health, it was delayed until January 10, 1889. By then, Louis had recovered sufficiently to be able to hold the arm of his "queen of Navarre" and escort her into the chapel, regally clothed as she was in a white bridal dress edged with soft, white ermine fur

7. Hénault-Morel, *Louis et Zélie Martin*, 241.
8. Hénault-Morel, 242.

and Alençon lace. It would be his last celebration with any of his daughters. Thérèse spoke of this day with prophetic words. It was "my King's day of triumph. I compare it to the entry of Jesus into Jerusalem on the day of the palms. Like that of our Divine Master, the glory of *a day* was followed by a painful passion and this passion was not his alone" (S 156).

A WAY IN WHICH YOU ENJOY NOT

Crisis Point

Almost immediately after this great day, Louis suffered several minor strokes that severely affected his mind. He started to have hallucinations of a violent and threatening nature, and on February 12, 1889, a crisis point was reached. Convinced that the Prussians had returned, "he thought he was seeing frightful things, slaughter and battles. He could hear the sound of cannons and drums."[9] To protect his daughters he armed himself with a revolver that he held ready in his hand. Céline described their awful situation: "Léonie and I were dumb, we kept silent all the time, we were exhausted, shattered, it really seemed to me that my heart was bleeding and that it was one big wound."[10]

It was time for a final and irreversible decision for Louis to be admitted into the regional psychiatric hospital in Caen, a large port on the Normandy coast. That same day Isidore arrived quickly to rescue his nieces. He disarmed his sixty-six-year-old brother-in-law and told him they were visiting Caen. Before leaving, Louis insisted on seeing his "pearl" at the Lisieux Carmel. In the parlor, he told her, "It's me, my Pauline, I'm bringing

---

9. Redmond, *Louis and Zélie Martin*, 253.

10. Clapier, *Louis et Zélie Martin*, 288.

you some fish," and then produced two or three little fish in his handkerchief.[11] Happy to join his brother-in-law on the forty-mile train journey, Louis thought he was going for a walk along the wide, sandy beach of Caen. A friend met them there and took Louis to the door of Bon Sauveur, the regional hospital for the mentally infirm. How did Louis feel when he realized where he was? This sensitive man had said the following about someone in Lisieux who was admitted into the psychiatric hospital in the same way: "It is the worst ordeal that a person can be subjected to."[12]

Hospital

At that time the Bon Sauveur, locally known as the "lunatic asylum," or more offensively, the "madhouse," instilled a mixture of terror and curiosity in the people of Caen. Originally a monastery, after the French Revolution it became a hospital for receiving the "alien spirits" (as mentally ill people were known), and then an institution for "debauched girls and women." Later, the Congregation of the Daughters of the Good Savior transformed it into a psychiatric hospital.[13] Admission could be initiated by the sick person's family but had to be supported by a medical practitioner.

Bon Sauveur, with all the facilities available on-site, was a village within itself. When Louis was admitted, more than two hundred and sixty religious and novices cared for six hundred

---

11. Clapier, 290.

12. Clapier, 290.

13. A law passed in 1838 decreed that every department (region) had to have an institution for the mentally ill, privately run but under the authority of the state.

or so mentally ill men and women, who were housed in separate complexes that catered to their respective conditions. The men's hospital complex was divided into eight sections, seven of which followed the classification of mental illnesses at that time: calm and semi-calm, senile and dirty, agitated, epileptic, and convalescent. The eighth section was for the nurses, children, and workers.

At that time, little was understood about the underlying pathology of insanity, but syphilis was suspected to cause "general paralysis of the insane," and alcohol to cause psychosis. "Idiots" (with a mental age of less than six years) and "imbeciles" (with a mental age of six to nine years) were included under the same umbrella. The Bon Sauveur Hospital, with its spacious buildings, dedicated nuns, and practical categorization of patients, was a remarkably enlightened and humane institution caring for this wide range of sick and marginalized human beings.

In addition, there were four hundred other patients, including those who were deaf and dumb. In total, 1,700 people lived on the spacious estate. Louis was assigned to St. Joseph, the section for the calmest patients, next to the hospital's chapel.

Bon Sauveur was known for its humanitarian methods, but there was little hope for any cures. The morning started at 5:00 a.m. (6:00 a.m. in winter) with prayer and breakfast in the refectory. Following the 7:00 a.m. Mass, patients worked according to their ability and were encouraged with allocations of tobacco, cigarettes, or small cash rewards. Louis helped with the construction of a pond facing the convent. He would have enjoyed the allocation of cider for the men who worked: three liters a day! Women were apparently deemed less thirsty; they were allocated one liter a day. After a break for lunch and recreation,

they worked until 5:00 p.m. and then had supper followed by
another recreation period, with games and a pipe or cigarette.
Night prayer and then bed at 8:00 p.m. (7:00 p.m. in winter)
brought the day to a close. The barber came once a month, and
patients had their hair cut every three months. Louis had always
enjoyed games such as chess and checkers at home, so in his
calm phases, would have been a good companion on those recreation evenings.

Humiliation

How did Louis respond to this loss of freedom and periods of
disorientation and distress? His dignity and bearing made him
stand out, but above all he was distinguished by his constant
belief that *everything* that happened to him was for the greater
glory of God. Sister Marie Adélaïde Costard oversaw the section
where Louis resided and said of him, "It is heart-breaking to see
this handsome patriarch in such a condition. We are sad, deeply
pained, and our staff is dismayed. In the short time that he has
been here, he has made himself loved, and, then, there is something so venerable about him. He bears no ordinary stamp. We
can see that it is a trial; it doesn't suit him to have this illness, and
this makes it all the more distressing."[14] In a letter to her Carmelite sisters, Céline showed how difficult it was for her father in
such a place: "He was very, very pleased with your letters. They
did him a lot of good; all day after having read them he was in
better spirits; he seemed to have new courage. They made him
see his condition as a trial of a great friend of God, and those
thoughts strengthen him."[15] Their father's acceptance was not

14. Redmond, *Louis and Zélie Martin*, 255.
15. Martin, *Father of the Little Flower*, 94.

because he found the illness and humiliation easy; he is a saint because it *was* hard and yet he allowed God's grace to accompany him and sustain him.

When the patient had a bad turn, he would cover his head with a blanket like a penitent, so fulfilling Thérèse's childhood premonition in what she called her "prophetic vision." As a child, she had been looking out of the window at Les Buissonnets when, to her alarm, she saw a stooped old man walking slowly across the garden: "His head was covered with a sort of apron of indistinct color and it hid his face" (S 46). When she and Céline rushed out to find him, no one was there. Now she realized this had been a premonition of her father's illness.

In a lucid moment, Louis told the doctor caring for him, "I have always been used to giving orders to others and to see myself reduced to obeying, it is hard. But I know why the good God has given me this trial. I have never had humiliation in my life and I need some."[16] In his response, the doctor told him there was yet more humiliation; Isidore Guérin had signed a power of attorney, taking over Louis's affairs. Louis was very distressed as he felt that not only his brother-in-law but also his children had abandoned him, that they no longer trusted him to make decisions.

Humiliation was not reserved for Louis, for his children were also vilified, both in the convent and in the streets of Lisieux. The Martin sisters, especially Thérèse, were blamed for causing their father's illness by callously leaving him for their own pious ends and abandoning him to the madhouse. Unwittingly adding insult to injury, the hospital doctor thought that the periods of agitation were a precursor of general paralysis, "otherwise

---

16. Clapier, *Louis et Zélie Martin*, 297.

known as syphilis, casting doubt on his morality or that of his preceding family."[17] These accusations born of ignorance heaped coals on the fire of humiliation for Louis and his daughters. One month later, Thérèse said, "I did not know that the 12 February, one month after I had taken the habit, our dear Father would drink the most bitter, the most humiliating of all cups."[18]

The Support of Family

To be near their father, Céline and Léonie became guests of the Sisters of St. Vincent de Paul, who had a convent near Bon Sauveur. They visited Louis every day, spending an hour with him in the parlor and then taking him for a walk in the gardens. He was looking forward to going back to Les Buissonnets very soon. But these periods of calm were succeeded by phases of agitation and hallucinations, and it was not safe to let him go home. After three months, Sister Costard told them that the regulations allowed visits only once a week, so Isidore advised them to come back to Lisieux and move in with his family, as the lease for Les Buissonnets had not been renewed and the contents were to be sold. This was the sorrowful end of an era for all the family.

Back in Lisieux, Léonie and Céline continued to visit their father by train every week. Occasionally, they went on vacation with their cousins, and so missed a visit. When Sister Costard explained this to Louis, he said, "Oh! how lovely! Tell them to stay there as long as their good uncle thinks best. I do not want them to return to Caen on my account. I am well, very well here."[19]

17. Hénault-Morel, *Louis et Zélie Martin*, 246.

18. Clapier, *Louis et Zélie Martin*, 287.

19. Martin, *Father of the Little Flower*, 97.

With only occasional breaks, the visiting routine took its toll, and in March 1891, Céline's health broke down. Her uncle and aunt suggested that she cut down on her visits since they caused her so much distress, and the doctor recommended especially that she avoid any emotional upsets. "Léonie and Céline then made few visits to Papa. There was very little they could do for him. Often, he was too sick to enjoy their visits, so much so that Léonie used to make use of the trip to Caen to call at the Visitation convent while Céline sat with Papa."[20] In time, their father's physical condition deteriorated further until both his legs were paralyzed, rendering him incapable of unpredictable actions and safe enough to come home in a wheelchair. The date was May 10, 1892; he had been at Bon Sauveur three years and three months.

A WAY OF PEACE

The last months

Louis was ensconced on the first floor of the Guérins' residence until Céline found a small house to rent, opposite her uncle's back garden, where she and Léonie could set up home with their father. However, in June 1893, Léonie went on a two-week retreat at the Visitation convent and stayed on to try her vocation again. Céline was understandably upset and angry to be thus left on her own, but her usual resilience took over (her father had after all called her the "intrepid"), and everyone joined forces to care for Louis.

By summer 1893, Isidore was determined that Louis would come with the family to La Musse, near Paris, where he had

---

20. Redmond, *Louis and Zélie Martin*, 261.

inherited a large house with 41 hectares of land, but getting him there seemed an insurmountable problem. How could they transport the wheelchair, invalid bed, and other luggage? The house was two miles from the station. Undaunted, Isidore managed to work out the transport arrangements, and Louis did indeed love the place. As Céline and her cousin, Marie Guérin, pushed his chair along the woodland paths, he was enraptured by the bird song and absorbed by the beautiful views. One evening he was entranced by a nightingale pouring out its rippling notes, and tears rolled down his cheeks.

After two months at La Musse, Céline and Marie came back with their beloved Louis to Lisieux, where the venerable patriarch was very content. He tended to take in more than his caregivers expected, as when they discussed replacing his rented wheelchair with a permanent one for purchase. To their surprise, he had followed their conversation and expressed immense delight when they found one. He loved to listen to the melodies played on the piano by his godchild, Marie. However, the gentle interlude was broken when Louis had another stroke in May 1894, serious enough for him to be given the last sacraments (confession, Holy Communion, and the sacrament of the sick). He seemed to be making a recovery, but nine days later he had a major heart attack. Although weak and barely able to swallow, his physical strength won through, and on July 5, the family was able to bring him to the house at La Musse for the last time. On July 28, Louis had a more severe heart attack and died at La Musse on July 29 at 8:15 in the morning. Céline was with him when he opened his eyes for the last time and gazed at her "with affection and inexpressible gratitude. His eyes were filled with life and understanding."[21]

21. Martin, *Father of the Little Flower*, 114.

Dementia: The End or the Beginning?

Blessed with the gift of words like her mother, Céline vividly describes the situation experienced by the families of those who have dementia: her despair and confusion, her loss of the strong father she knew, the total change in her lifestyle, and her sense of isolation and abandonment. But she also experienced what many people describe: a certainty that God was mysteriously involved in all the pain.

Although it was tragic to see their dear father wearing the institutional clothes and at times locked in to prevent him wandering off, Léonie and Céline must have been amazed at his spirit and the way his caregivers loved him. Sister Costard said of him, "This venerable old man only speaks of the great glory of God! He is truly admirable. Not only does he never complain, but he finds everything one gives him excellent. When he is given something special, there is gratitude without end."[22] Unless having a disturbed spell, Louis made it a pleasure for the staff to help him and would share everything with the other patients, even a gift of his favorite delicacy, fresh Normandy oysters.

Here we see a vocation within a vocation. Louis had always grasped the different phases of his life with both hands: each stage was a new challenge, a new vocation. He followed through his first calling to be a monk as far as he felt he could, but that life was not for him. The second calling was to be a watchmaker, and the third a husband to Zélie. He then realized that his fourth vocation was to be a father to his children, the fifth a businessman for the Alençon lace, and the sixth to be a single parent. His last juncture in life was the answer to his prayer

22. Hénault-Morel, *Louis et Zélie Martin*, 247.

to give everything—being called to be a person with vascular dementia and an in-patient in a psychiatric hospital.

Louis entered fully into his hospital existence. His relationship with God overflowed into his relationships on the ward with his caregivers and fellow patients alike; it shone through in this situation as in all his previous stages of life. "God in his great glory" was his raft on the choppy seas of dementia. In the muddle of his mind, he could repeat those words with blind faith. Louis's story also portrays some challenges of physical disabilities that necessitate dependence on a wheelchair. Isidore's sheer determination to overcome all obstacles to get his brother-in-law to the countryside (without a car!) is something that will resonate with many caregivers.

The most poignant sadness of seeing someone you love gradually lose their mind is the unmentionable sense of loss. The human being we knew seems to die before death takes him or her away. Those with advanced dementia seem to exist in an anteroom of the next world, and perhaps that is what it is. For Louis and those who cared for him, faith in a God who cares, who is involved and who understands, was the God they came to know. No longer was he the bookkeeping God of retributive justice. Louis did not suffer the indignity of his final years to "earn" his place in heaven. He was asked by God to live out his final vocation as a gift for all those who follow him on the path of dementia, to go by the way in which they are not.

QUESTIONS FOR REFLECTION

- Do you have elderly relatives to care for? How does your love for them bring your family into a deeper union with God's love for people who are weak and frail?

- If you are approaching old age or any debilitating condition, does it fill you with fear and sadness, or do you see it as a new calling given by God to trust him even more deeply?

- Have you ever felt thoroughly humiliated and misjudged for something that was outside your control? Who or what helped you through this time, and can it now be seen as a gift from God rather than a depressing memory?

11

The Spirituality of Marriage

The kingdom of heaven is like a mustard seed that someone took and sowed in his field; it is the smallest of all the seeds, but when it has grown it is the greatest of shrubs and becomes a tree, so that the birds of the air come and make nests in its branches.

—MATTHEW 13:31–32

The Least of All Seeds

So too your kingdom comes: a single seed
Too tiny to be seen, sown in the womb,
And then sown deeper still, to meet our need,
A second sowing in the stone cold tomb.
Till in your spring and growth, alive and free,
You raise us to the branches of your tree.

—MALCOLM GUITE, PARABLE AND PARADOX[1]

---

1. "The Least of All Seeds" is taken from *Parable and Paradox: Sonnets on the Sayings of Jesus and Other Poems* by Malcolm Guite (Norwich, UK: Canterbury, 2016).

TINY IS MIGHTY

The Seed of the Kingdom of Heaven

In this parable, it is astonishing that Jesus likened the kingdom of heaven to such an insignificant item: a mustard seed "too tiny to be seen." The parable is made more powerful by revealing that the greatest kingdom imaginable grows from a *single* seed, a miniscule germ of life enabled to fulfill its potential by one humble person who has sown it in the soil. Hundreds of seeds and teams of people are not required to inaugurate the kingdom of heaven; all that is needed is the response of the individual heart to the touch of God. It is also a wonder to see that it was another tiny thing, a stitch of lace, that brought Louis and Zélie together, when Louis's mother came to know Zélie at the school for *point d'Alençon*. In her maternal wisdom, she recognized the inner beauty of the young woman and opened the eyes of Louis, her last remaining child, to the vocation of marriage.

The marriage of the lace-maker and watchmaker, launched by an instant glance of mutual recognition on a bridge in Alençon, continues to reverberate in our world today. Their love for each other was sown by God's compassionate love in the field of their being, in the soil of their marriage.

The Family's Mission

With their roots ever deepening in their vocation to marriage, Louis and Zélie formed a trunk of strength from which their branches reached out to the world. The *mission* of their marriage was to provide nesting places for the "birds of the air," the many people who came in and out of the busy home in Alençon, and people of all races and nationalities who have since come to know Louis and Zélie Martin and their daughters, especially Thérèse. From one seed, a family tree burgeoned for all to find a branch to nest their souls, a place to feel at home.

However, before reaching out to the world, Louis and Zélie founded a family, a community. Pope St. John Paul II, in his apostolic exhortation *Familiaris Consortio* (On the Role of the Christian Family in the Modern World), in 1981, reinforced the concept of a mission that starts at home:

> The family has the *mission* to become more and more what it is, that is to say, a *community of life and love*, in an effort that will find fulfillment, as will everything created and redeemed, in the Kingdom of God. Looking at it in such a way as to reach its very roots, we must say that the essence and role of the family are in the final analysis specified by love. Hence the family has the mission to guard, reveal, and communicate love, and this is a living reflection of and a real sharing in God's love for humanity and the love of Christ the Lord for the church His bride. (FC 17, emphasis added)

It sounds too good to be true, but everything that the members of the family do for each other and with each other, in generosity and love, is nothing less than participation in God's love for humanity.

This mystery of participation is trumpeted not in great lights and visions but in the give and take of ordinary families, living ordinary lives. Louis and Zélie Martin lived this mystery. In their time, no one thought the Martin household was particularly exceptional. True, they were hardworking, one could set one's watch by the sound of their door closing every morning as they left for church, and they involved themselves in parish life and joined Catholic fraternities—but many other Catholic families lived likewise in their provincial town. What was different about the Martin family?

Zélie opened her first letter to her brother with the words, "God protects all who trust in Him. Not a single person has ever been abandoned by Him" (CF 1). She thus spelled out the foundation of the family she and Louis would bring into the world: a foundation of faith in a caring and involved Father who would hold the family safe through everything that was going to come. With God's help, she and Louis would create a "community of life and love" as Pope John Paul describes.

Support from Others

The core of this community for Louis and Zélie was their family, and the wider community included relations, friends, those who worked for them, the needy in Alençon, and fellow parishioners. These fellow travelers were involved in their work, leisure, education, friendships, prayer, and childcare, providing Louis and Zélie with a rich companionship for their marriage. It is hard, if not impossible, for two people alone to commit themselves to stay together for the rest of their lives, "for richer, for poorer, in sickness and in health," but support and affirmation from others helps to strengthen the couple's relationship. Louis and Zélie's commitment to each other was made rich and fruitful through their relationship with those around them. So too, couples today find fulfillment of their marriage vows through their family, friends, church, neighbors, and work colleagues, to name but a few.

This fulfillment is not a one-way process. No one can constantly give to others without being nourished in their turn, or they will become exhausted and disheartened. We are asked by Jesus to love each other *as we love ourselves* (Mt 19:19). To give as generously as they did to others, Louis and Zélie took care to nurture their own spiritual lives. Pope St. Paul VI in his Decree on the Apostolate of the Laity (*Apostolicam Actuositatem*) tells us that, in the varying circumstances of their life, individuals "should remember, nevertheless, that man is naturally social and that it has pleased God to unite those who believe in Christ into the people of God" (AA 18). Through these "people of God" in the Catholic Church, Louis and Zélie, and later their children, found a channel of strength and encouragement. The sacrament of the Eucharist was their priority, but the various groups and confraternities to which they belonged gave them a structure within which they were *active* in outreach to others and *contemplative* in prayer shared with fellow parishioners.

Through the St. Vincent de Paul Society, Louis unobtrusively helped destitute people in Alençon. Céline gives one example: "We had been out for a walk in the country when, as we neared the town, my father went into a home which we did not recognize but which seemed well-known to him."[2] Louis then gave money to the woman, who was alone with her two small children, explaining to Céline that he helped her out when her husband abandoned her from time to time.

THE POWER OF PRAYER

Prayer of the Church

Active as Louis and Zélie were in Alençon, the influence of their marriage was already spreading further than they could have envisaged. As a pebble dropped into a lake sends out concentric

---

2. Martin, *Father of the Little Flower*, 24.

ripples that disappear into the distance, the witness of their marriage based on faith in a loving God has now spread far and wide. This "ripple effect" continues to be true for all Christian families. "The Church of the home is also called to be a luminous sign of the presence of Christ and of His love for those who are 'far away,' for families who do not yet believe, and for those Christian families who no longer live in accordance with the faith that they once received" (FC 54).[3] How does a Christian family do this? They can do so by simply letting God be not a distant critic of their self-perceived inadequacies but *part* of their family life.

The sacrament of marriage is ongoing; it is God's leaven that raises up every part of every day. Pope Francis reassures us in his apostolic exhortation *Amoris Laetitia* (The Joy of Love) that "neither of the spouses will be alone in facing whatever challenges come their way. Both are called to respond to God's gift with commitment, creativity, perseverance and daily effort. They can always invoke the assistance of the Holy Spirit who consecrated their union, so that his grace may be felt in every new situation that they encounter" (AL 74).

Every new day brings new situations, however repetitive and routine such activities as the school run or daily commute may be. Whether a smile across the kitchen table or quietly emptying the dishwasher, small generous acts of everyday life can be sacramental signs of God's presence, of his love at the heart of the family. Through the "assistance of the Holy Spirit who consecrated their union," Christian parents are one with the church in this sacramental expression of the demands of family life. The

---

3. See also "The Heart of the Deepest Truth," World Bishops' Message to Families, Rome, October 25, 1980, para. 14.

following poem, with its refrain from an old African American lullaby sung in the South, expresses this beautifully:

Vowed to This Life

We face each other across the choir
in the night cathedral of our married lives
summoned by an infant's hungry wail
to chant the hours after Compline.

Hush, little baby, don't say a word . . .

We recite the old antiphonies
that keep at bay the terrors of the dark:
"I checked. You're safe. I'm sure.
There are no monsters under the bed."
We rise for the Nocturnes, the watches
of the night, observe the mercury rising,
proffer cool ablutions. ". . . a hundred and four.
Yes, certainly, we can bring him in."

Sent for the doctor / The doctor said . . .

Through the night the porch light burns in vigil.
Past midnight we sleep lightly, half waiting
for a ring that cracks the stillness of the hour:
"This is Officer Olsen. Are you the parent . . ."
We are caught up lifelong in the liturgy
of the hours, called to Matins by the ringing
in the dark, groping for the phone.
"Mom, the baby won't stop crying."

Hush, little baby, don't say a word . . .

When the birds begin their chorus
and the sun lights up the east
we're back to bed for consolation
and then we rise for Lauds.[4]

These verses vividly describe how Louis and Zélie engaged with the prayer of the church, the daily "Hours" of the Divine Office at morning (Lauds), evening (Compline), and during the night (Nocturnes and Matins). Their dawn walks to see their sick babies, nursing their sick children through the night, and coping with a child's impossible behavior are just some examples Zélie has given through her letters.

Parents today are also invited to participate in this cycle of prayer with the church. Getting up in the middle of the night, nursing a newborn baby, changing diapers, walking the floor with colicky little ones, and then later consoling tearful teens who failed the team or broke up with a boyfriend—all these things are truly sacramental. They are reflections of God's love in the family, though they may not feel like it at the time. They point to an astonishing union in prayer within the family of the church: those praying the Divine Office every second somewhere in the world are in union in prayer with parents who, every second somewhere, are "caught up lifelong in the liturgy of the hours," as the above poem says. Its title, "Vowed to This Life," expresses a deep reality.

Elizabeth of the Trinity took this concept of the shared cloister to a more profound level when she wrote to Antoinette, a busy mother with small children, "Oh yes, may the God who is all love be your unchanging dwelling place, your cell, and your

---

4. Mary Kay Schoen, "Vowed to This Life," *America: The Jesuit Review*, September 19, 2011. Emphasis added.

cloister in the midst of the world" (L 261). This inner sanctum is within every parent, waiting to be entered, especially, Elizabeth adds, "when you sense your weakness, go to Him; He is the Strong One" (L 261).

The Eucharist

This lifelong liturgy of family life is particularly sacramental when nurtured by the sacraments of the church. The ongoing grace from the sacrament of marriage flows as a deep undercurrent, but for the ebb and flow of each day, Louis and Zélie found their strength and direction through their participation in daily Mass. They joined the workers of Alençon in hearing the Word of God and, when possible, in receiving Christ in the Blessed Sacrament. The Eucharist was the rudder that guided and stabilized the family boat, however threatening the waves.

Each day started with Mass, and reception of Holy Communion as often as the custom allowed. Receiving Christ's precious Body was a very special event for which preparations were made with great care. "I never miss, nor does Marie and, naturally, nor does Louis, receiving Communion every First Friday of the month, no matter what difficulties we foresee for that day. We change the time of the Mass we usually go to, and that's all that's needed" (CF 140). It was something to write about, as Louis wrote to Zélie from a business trip to Paris for the Alençon lace: "I had the happiness of receiving Communion at Notre-Dame des Victoires, which is like a little heaven on earth" (CF 2-a). Before she had made her first Holy Communion, the youngest child, Thérèse, also wanted to be part of this special event; she would pester Céline on her return from the Sunday service to give her the "special bread" so she could have "my Mass" (S 26).

Zélie did not leave the preparation of the children for First Holy Communion to the school or parish catechist but taught them from her own experience. She wrote several very beautiful letters of instruction to Marie at boarding school, which Marie treasured so much that she brought them home in the holidays. Unfortunately, Louise, the maid, mistook the bundle for waste paper and used the letters to light the fire (CF 47n118). However, her letters bore rich fruit, as Zélie said: "I'm very happy that Marie has made her First Communion, despite her young age.[5] If you knew how well-prepared she was; she looked like a little saint" (CF 47).

Regarding her more wayward daughter, Zélie told her sister-in-law who was asking what New Year's presents the children would like, "As for Léonie, you could give her a rosary for her First Communion, which she'll make on the Feast of the Holy Trinity. She knows her catechism perfectly and answers the questions better than I would have believed" (CF 125). Zélie seemed pleasantly surprised. However, she was quick to notice if the desire to receive Jesus in the Blessed Sacrament was more about wearing a pretty white dress. "I must take Léonie to the Catechism class on perseverance. But this is the last time, because her Second Solemn Communion[6] will take place on Sunday, May 21 [1876]. As always, Léonie is looking forward to being all in white. Up until now the material side strikes her more than the spiritual" (CF 159).

---

5. The date was moved forward as Zélie's sister, Sister Dosithée, was terminally ill with tuberculosis.

6. The grand celebration of a Second Solemn Communion was made when a child reached the age of reason, after their First Communion. In France, this custom persisted until the 1970s.

Sundays: Daring to Be Different

First Communion was a big family occasion, but each Sunday was also very special for the children. Thérèse wrote, "If the big feasts were rare, each week brought one that was very dear to my heart, namely Sunday! What a day Sunday was for me! It was God's feast day, and feast of *rest*" (S 41). As the baby of the family, she slept in, and then Pauline brought her hot chocolate in bed before brushing and curling her long, golden hair. There was no school, and after a heavenly High Mass, the family enjoyed long walks in the countryside. It was a day of physical and spiritual treats. The evening brought song and laughter round the fire but naturally with some individual preferences, as Zélie exclaimed: "[Sunday evening], Marie wants donuts, others want cake, and others chestnuts, but as for me, I would like peace" (CF 146).

It was a challenge then, as it is now, to keep Sundays as a Christian day of rest. Writing to her sister-in-law, Zélie said, "As for me, I'm going to be careful not to buy anything on Sunday anymore. I'm not as strict about this as you and my husband are. For example, when I need a small loaf of bread for my children, I have it bought" (CF 140). French bread then, as today, became hard after one day.

If possible, Louis and Zélie avoided encouraging people to work on Sundays, even regarding travel. This could create quite a dilemma, as when Zélie managed to escape from work to visit her brother in Lisieux for a few days but could not get away on the Saturday, as she explained to him: "It's impossible for me to leave on Saturday this time, and on Sunday, I can't travel all morning. That would be against my principles because I believe that we have to be very careful not to contribute to work on Sunday" (CF 74). She got around it in her mind by catching the train at 3:30 a.m. on Sunday morning. This seems a hard act to follow, and unlike her husband, Zélie did indeed feel some conflict in following these awkward expectations made on them as sincere Catholics.

CREATIVE ENERGY

Spiritual Freedom

Spiritual nourishment was provided through the parish by the daily Eucharist, parish groups, pilgrimages, and processions, but Louis and Zélie also sought out individual spiritual guidance. Louis went to the Trappist monastery in Soligny-la-Trappe, about thirty miles east of Alençon, for silent weekend retreats.[7] In the peace of the monastic cycle of prayer, he could become more deeply aware of the still, small voice of God that guided him throughout his family life. Zélie's spiritual home was the Franciscan convent in Alençon. As a Third Order Franciscan and a member of the Archconfraternity of Christian Mothers, she met there every month, but she also saw the Poor Clares for spiritual direction and to ask for their prayers. They were like an extended family, for they knew of her family problems and challenges: the death of her babies, her father's final illness, and her difficulties with Léonie. She could be quite specific in her requests, as when, delighted to hear that her brother had passed his exams, she told him, "You know, I contributed a little to your success because I asked the Poor Clares in Alençon to pray for you Wednesday and Thursday at 10:00 in the morning, thinking it was the time of your exams" (CF 3).

---

7. Founded in 1122 and destroyed during the French Revolution, it was rebuilt in 1832. The Trappist monks were expelled by antireligious laws in 1880, but they returned after two years and the monastery continues to offer a place of prayer.

Vocational Guidance

As they got older, the children too benefited from inspiring Jesuit priests who gave school retreats and individual guidance. These spiritual guides helped the girls understand what God was asking of them, often to the surprise of their mother. For example, Zélie, knowing that Pauline wanted to be a religious, had assumed that she would join her aunt as a nun at the Visitation convent, but following a retreat, Pauline announced that her vocation was in fact to be a Carmelite.

Regarding Marie, both parents thought she was too worldly and independent to enter a convent. Zélie described how, when Marie was sixteen, "one day when she was wearing a new outfit for the first time, could you believe she went into the garden and cried, saying that we dressed her like a young girl whom we wanted to marry off at all costs, and that it would certainly be because of us that she would be asked! . . . I don't think she'll ever get married, although she doesn't seem to have a religious vocation" (CF 161). However, she noticed a difference after Marie went on a retreat, saying, "Marie is completely changed since her retreat. It seems the Jesuit priest who gave it is a saint" (CF 163). Another Jesuit priest, Father Almire Pichon, became Marie's spiritual director and a friend of all the family. The wisdom of all these experienced spiritual guides, Trappists, Franciscans, and Jesuits, helped the children to develop inner spiritual freedom and make their own decisions when it came to leaving the nest.

Although they were not constrained by a need to conform to their parents' wishes, the children were deeply influenced by the way their parents lived with total trust in God and his Blessed Mother as part of their daily existence. Each day brought external observances such as going to Mass, but equally important were the observances at home. Morning and night prayers, like bedtime stories, were not just a duty but also special times of the day spent with their mother, and with their father after she died. Thus, from an early age, the girls became aware of the presence of Jesus in this world and in heaven. For a moving example, during the last few weeks of their mother's life, Céline and Thérèse were sent off each day to stay with their cousin (Louis's nephew to whom he sold his watchmaking business). One day, having forgotten to say their morning prayers, their cousin's wife left them in a large room where they could say them. Céline looked in dismay at her sister saying, "Oh! This is not like Mama! She always had us say our prayers with her" (S 33). The Martin family was a small community of people who worked, prayed, and learned together.

The Domestic Church

Pope St. John Paul II, in *Familiaris Consortio* (On the Role of the Christian Family in the Modern World), describes the concept of a family's togetherness lived in the spirit of Christ as "the little domestic church, like the greater church" that has a duty to constantly grow in knowledge of its faith (FC 51). The Martin family shows us that this domestic church is nothing grand; it is a place, a family unit, where service and generosity are built upon trust in a loving God and nourished by the sacraments and an appetite for understanding the faith.

Regarding their involvement in their children's education, First Holy Communions, pilgrimages, and prayer in the parish and the family, Louis and Zélie were ahead of their time. The World Bishops' Message to Families in 1980 said, "In fulfilling these tasks the family will be, as it were a 'domestic church,' a community of faith living in hope and love, serving God and the entire human family. Shared prayer and the liturgy are sources of grace for families. In fulfilling its tasks the family must nourish itself on God's word and participate in the life of the sacraments, especially reconciliation and the Eucharist. Traditional and contemporary devotions, particularly those associated with the Blessed Virgin, are rich sources of growth in piety and grace."[8] Pope Francis mentions this concept again in *Amoris Laetitia* (The Joy of Love), saying, "The family lives its spirituality precisely by being at one and the same time a domestic church and a vital cell for transforming the world" (AL 324).

Within the domestic church of the home there is a profound truth. The Catechism of the Catholic Church points out that "it is here that the father of the family, the mother, children and all members of the family exercise the *priesthood of the baptized* in a privileged way" (CCC 1657). Louis and Zélie held priests in reverence as representatives of God but may not have recognized how they themselves were exercising their baptismal priesthood "by the reception of the sacraments, prayer and thanksgiving, the witness of a holy life, and self-denial and active charity" (CCC 1657). Put into everyday parlance, *everyone* in the Christian family can be a priest through their baptism by thanking God and offering to him all the joys, challenges, and sufferings of family life, and by living their faith to the full. Pope St. John Paul II brings this home when he says in *Familiaris Consortio* (On the Role of the Christian Family in the Modern World), "This is the priestly role which the Christian family can and ought to exercise in intimate communion with the whole Church, through the daily realities of married and family life" (FC 55).

---

8. "Heart of the Deepest Truth," para. 13.

THE PARADOX OF MARRIAGE

A Second Sowing

In their relatively short married life together, Louis and Zélie's relationship with God was honed by suffering. They underwent the pain of having to watch the suffering and death of their children without knowing how to help them, and Louis had to watch his wife suffer and call out in agony until she too died. As we do to this day, they lived with the reality of sickness, war, old age, and death. But their sufferings did not make them withdraw into sad isolation; they did not wallow in a quagmire of "why me?" In fact, they were quite open about how they felt, whether sad, confused, anxious, or annoyed. Louis does not present as a "hard" man; on the contrary, like St. Paul, his strength lay in his vulnerability (see 2 Cor 12:9). Both he and Zélie found real strength in being honest about how they felt. Paradoxically, the end of their married life together, the second sowing of the seed "in the stone cold tomb," would lead to new life in a strange and counterintuitive way.

Paradox is God's way of bringing us through something that seems to be a block. Christ asked his Father that he might come *through* his passion and cross to his resurrection. So also in this marriage of Louis and Zélie, we see transformations through seemingly terrible situations. Repeated bereavements brought them an ever deeper awareness of God's loving care. A desire for purity and celibacy was redirected into the fertility of family. The child who was the most perplexing problem became the greatest stimulus to transformation. A man of mental prowess delved into the depths of God's mercy through losing his intellect. The woman who rejoiced in motherhood was asked to leave her children when they needed her most. The crucible of suffering became the crucible of creation, as the last two lines of Malcolm Guite's sonnet promise:

> Till in your spring and growth, alive and free,
> You raise us to the branches of your tree.

Louis and Zélie Martin show us that, whatever befalls a man or woman in their married life, God has it all in hand. They show us that love at the heart of the family is something alive and active. It is expressed in joy and delight or sorrow and pain, as all these are signs of caring for another, feelings that reflect love. In his apostolic exhortation on love in the family, Pope Francis tells us,

> We have always spoken of how God dwells in the hearts of those living in his grace. Today we can add that the Trinity is present in the temple of marital communion.
>
> The Lord's presence dwells in real and concrete families, with all their daily troubles and struggles, joys and hopes. . . . The spirituality of family love is made up of thousands of small but real gestures. (AL 314–15)

Saints for Today

With God dwelling in the heart of the family, every event in that family's life is raised up to him like the branches of the growing mustard tree reaching up to heaven. Anything is possible. Louis and Zélie Martin are saints for every parent struggling to raise a family, every woman longing for a child, everyone suffering from terminal illness, every caregiver of a loved one with dementia, and every mother or father bringing up children on their own. Louis and Zélie are saints for moms and dads when they are dismayed, ashamed, feeling an inadequate "failure," depressed, or afraid, for Louis and Zélie were not ashamed to tell their family how they felt. There is no experience in these situations that cannot be sacramental with a small *s*, a sign of God's grace and love. The man and the woman who walked into that church in Alençon at midnight to get married lived their family life to the full and are now telling the world. Their welcoming branches are for all to find a nest for their souls, a place to feel at home. Now is the time for the sacrament of marriage to reach its full potential through the witness of an ordinary husband and wife, Louis and Zélie Martin.

QUESTIONS FOR REFLECTION

• What is the mission of your marriage? Has the original vision changed with circumstances, and does this bring joy or sorrow? Does your faith in your marriage as an ongoing sacrament help in any way?

• When you as a couple reach out to others and offer a place of welcome, do you see it as participation in God's love for all humanity? How could this realization deepen your awareness of God's presence in your marriage?

• How does your family form a community? How does this give the children sound roots in faith and freedom to discover their own paths in life?

12

Gathering Up
the Fragments

*Then Jesus took the loaves, and when he had given thanks,
he distributed them to those who were seated; so also the
fish, as much as they wanted. When they were satisfied, he
told his disciples, "Gather up the fragments left over, so that
nothing may be lost." So they gathered them up, and from
the fragments of the five barley loaves, left by those who
had eaten, they filled twelve baskets.*

—JOHN 6:11–13

NOTHING IS LOST

Everyone feels fragmented at times. "I feel torn to bits," we say
when a situation leaves us exhausted and emotional. "My life was
in shreds," we relate, when remembering the outcome of a cata-
strophic event. "I feel torn apart," we say, when people we love
pull us in two directions. If only we could remain in one piece,
whole and wholesome.

Through their experiences, Louis and Zélie show us how
God is active in our own family lives. Unless Jesus had broken
into pieces the five little loaves he accepted from a small boy,

he could not have fed the five thousand "who were seated." So too he takes not only the successes but also the shreds and fragments of our lives and transforms them in ways beyond our understanding. He accepts our tiniest and seemingly "childish" offerings to feed an infinitesimal number of people we will never know. Our hidden heroisms provide sustenance not only to our own families but also through them and future generations to myriad unknown people who are looking for encouragement and strength, who are hungry for help when facing trials in their family life. Indeed, he gathers up the fragments left over from our efforts and shattering experiences so that nothing may be lost, just as the potter wastes none of the "spoiled" clay but reworks it to make a fine pot. God values those very aspects of ourselves and our lives that we tend to ridicule and feel ashamed about, that we see as "failures." They are the very places where he is to be found.

To conclude, let us review how Louis and Zélie reveal the way in which God tenderly and actively cares for those who embark on the sacrament of marriage.

REVIEW OF A MARRIAGE

Louis and Zélie Martin show us that, while big events stand out, it is the small, even hesitant steps of the journey in married life that God values and magnifies. These two individuals were not strangers to hesitation, for we have seen how they were shaped by their respective childhoods before meeting each other, and how these experiences influenced the early months of marriage. When they started their own family together, each was influenced by their finely honed patterns of coping with life and responding to God's will.

Zélie, having buried her need for love and nurture under strength of mind and caring for others, assumed she would give her life to God as a professed nun. Instead she forged her independence through lace-making and discovered her true vocation through a caring husband and the delight of motherhood. But the delight soon melded with tragedy, loss, and then her own death. Louis, having seen all his siblings die, wanted nothing more than to give himself to God as a monk in the mountains but discovered a gift for making fine watches and clocks. He subsumed his monastic desire into a "pure" marriage but then opened his heart to the pleasures and pains of normal marriage and family life.

Exposure to the shocking events of their time, both locally and nationally, brought fear for the children, fear of penury, and even fear of going to war, but through all these alarms and anxieties Louis and Zélie developed an ever-deepening trust in God that in turn empowered their inner resources and strengthened their love for each other.

This couple were also exposed to personal tragedies that changed their lives. While both had unwavering faith in God's goodness, neither Zélie nor her husband approached her terminal cancer with holy joy or pious oblivion. They, as people do today, experienced fear, questioning, desire to protect their family, and a desperate need to *do* something.

Through their trials and tribulations, Louis and Zélie discovered that they had no power to "earn" anything from God, whether it was the gift of children, a peaceful death, or a secure place in heaven. They reversed the notion that God gives us suffering to punish us and discovered that God suffers *with* us and in us. Their experience would lead them into the cracks and crevices of future suffering parents and penetrate the pain of modern mothers and fathers with deep understanding and compassion. From the sickness and death of their infants to their own sickness and death from cancer and dementia, this couple have lived through and understand many of our own shattering experiences. They too were afflicted by grief, fear, anxiety, darkness, and near despair. They, as parents today, tried very hard to do things right, but the gentle hands of God remolded the things that were "wrong" to make them into even more beautiful earthenware pots.

Louis and Zélie also give us a way of managing the more mundane aspects of married life. In their use of money and their struggles with work-life balance, they demonstrate how marriage is the means by which God works with us. Their wealth provided dowries for their children, helped out relatives, and gave employees a fair wage; it provided care for the sick, food for the hungry, and shoes and clothing for those without. "God's portion" set aside for charity kept the finances in perspective; money was God's gift and to be used with good sense and generosity.

Further, Louis and Zélie give witness to the way in which the transforming effect of parenting dissolves our dreams and replaces them with realities that make us strong. We have seen how Léonie lived out the life of a misunderstood and suffering child, from her infancy eczema to her adolescent "terrible" behavior and her repeated failures at school. One could say that she represents all children who are difficult or very sick. These children, who do not or cannot make the parenting experience immediately rewarding, free parents from the need to be "perfect." Through them, their parents are led to discover God in the hidden hollows of helplessness, pain, and bewilderment, the hidden hollows of heroism. As a parent of a child with special needs discovers, their fight for their vulnerable child brings out a strength they never knew they had.

In spite of the difficulties, the strongest message that shines through this couple's story is expressed by the joy and fulfillment their children gave them. Both found a new purpose to life; they were filled with the delight of sharing in their children's lives, watching them put down roots and grow new branches reaching out into the world.

Louis demonstrated how his gifts came to light and flourished as he faced the challenge of raising five girls as a single father. After his "pearl" Pauline, his "diamond" Marie, and then his "queen of Navarre" Thérèse left him in turn to join the Carmelite convent, he was sad but not dismayed. On the contrary, filled with the joy of having had a full and happy life, he entered the unknown territory of his final vocation: to lose his most treasured possession, his mind.

This couple give an example of holy, wholesome parenthood, not due to honeyed achievements but because their ideals, their self-images, and even their notions of a judgmental God had to be *broken* for new life to emerge. This fragmentation, far from destroying them, released new strengths and a stronger relationship with each other and with their children.

SAINTS

In the story of Louis and Zélie, there is much to admire and, from our modern knowledge of child-rearing, aspects to criticize. We are drawn to some aspects of their personalities but may feel nothing in common with other traits. As saints, how can Louis and Zélie be "good models" of marriage and family life for us today?

This is a natural question, but is it the right question? It is a mistake to try to take a saint as our model because the Holy Spirit takes on so many guises in people, each unique. All people respond to the Holy Spirit by being *truly* themselves. We're not called to be carbon copies of others but to allow the Holy Spirit the freedom to work with us, as his instrument in the world. We are listening to what the Holy Spirit is saying to us *now*. We are called to the same level of self-giving as the saint but not to copy the saint.

A saint has an inner certitude of mission and of love, which invade the soul and grow together. The Holy Spirit calls, inspires, and changes people to become disciples of Jesus in *their* time. Louis and Zélie walked their paths together in total commitment. Through their relationship, they fulfilled their joint mission in marriage and entered into a deeper love than either could have envisaged, the love of God for every human being.

This couple offers us an insight into the vocation of marriage. Placing them on a pedestal of impossible holiness would do them a disservice, but understanding how God worked through their lives gives us a window into how God is present in our marriages and our families. Through their experience, they are witnesses and a source of encouragement at this time of history. They plunge into the depths of their vocation to marriage and open it up to the needs of people today.

MISSION OF MARRIAGE TODAY

Marriage is a mystery of participation in God's love for humanity. Anything a parent undergoes gives a little insight into God's patience, perseverance, and respect for every individual he has created. Like the small boy at the Feeding of the Five Thousand, we too can offer our Lord the little loaves we try to make in our marriages, our relationships, and our family lives, and allow him to multiply the fruits of our efforts a thousandfold. We can be sure that God looks on all our endeavors, messy and inadequate as they are, with huge compassion and great love and appreciation for what good is in them, however little it might seem. Indeed, he works through and with our struggles despite our limitations. Our strivings to follow a career, our anxious waiting for a baby, and our bedside vigils by a sick child or parent are all a part of the mystery of redemption.

As Louis and Zélie were energized by incorporating God's care and love into their family life, so too God longs for his love and care to be absorbed by families today, with all their hurts and fears, misunderstandings and sorrows, and celebrations and sharing. Not only where there is joy, but also where there is anguish—that is precisely where he is waiting. He will transform the heartache into a source of growth and new life if we let him. He awaits, in all humility, our permission for him to transform our lives through ordinary family events, to make each person the unique saint he or she is created to be.

Louis and Zélie have been given to us by the church to be friends of all families, because they have been through the experience of family life in joy and tragedy themselves. They will understand and intercede for every man and woman who turns to them for help on their own journeys in marriage and family life.

QUESTIONS FOR REFLECTION

- Are there events in your marriage, or that of your parents or friends, that seemed to be disastrous at the time but, looking back, reveal God's intervention?
- How have these events changed the family members involved?
- How can you bring Louis and Zélie Martin into your family life as friends and intercessors for your family's needs?

PERMISSIONS

The Scripture quotations contained herein are from the New Revised Standard Version Bible: Catholic Edition, copyright 1989 by the Division of Christian Education of the National Council of the Churches of Christ in the USA and are used by permission. All rights reserved.

Gracewing, Leominster, UK, for a quotation from *Saint Thérèse of Lisieux and Her Sisters* by Jennifer Moorcroft (2014).

Hymns Ancient and Modern for a quotation from *Parable and Paradox: Sonnets on the Sayings of Jesus and Other Poems* by Malcolm Guite (Norwich, UK: Canterbury, 2016).

Les Éditions du Cerf, Paris, for quotations from *Louis et Zélie Martin* by Thierry Hénault-Morel (2015).

Our Sunday Visitor, Huntington, Ind., for a quotation from *The Extraordinary Parents of St. Thérèse of Lisieux* by Hélène Mongin, translated by Marsha Daigle-Williamson. (2015).

Presses de la Renaissance, Paris, for quotations from *Louis et Zélie Martin: Une sainteté pour tous les temps* by Jean Clapier (2009).

Quiller Press, London, for quotations from *Louis and Zélie Martin: The Seed and the Root of the Little Flower* by Paulinus Redmond (1995).

Mary Kay Schoen for her poem "Vowed to This Life," quoted in *America: The Jesuit Review*, September 19, 2011.

Society of St. Paul, New York, for many quotations from *A Call to a Deeper Love: The Family Correspondence of the Parents of Saint Thérèse of the Child Jesus, 1863–1885*, by Zélie and Louis Martin, edited by Frances Renda, translated by Ann Connors Hess (2011).

St. Benedict Press/TAN Books, Charlotte, N.C., for quotations from *The Father of the Little Flower* by Céline Martin, translated by Michael Collins (2005); and from *The Story of a Family: The Home of St. Thérèse of Lisieux* by Stéphane-Joseph Piat, translated by a Benedictine of Stanbrook Abbey (2015).

Veritas Publications, Dublin, for quotations from *Léonie Martin: A Difficult Life* by Marie Baudouin-Croix (1993).

Archives of Lisieux Carmel: *http://www.archives-carmel-lisieux.fr/*.

BIBLIOGRAPHY

Baudouin-Croix, Marie. *Léonie Martin: A Difficult Life*. Dublin: Veritas, 1993.

Blommestjin, Hein, Jos Huls, and Kees Waaijman. *The Footprints of Love: John of the Cross as Guide in the Wilderness*. Translated by John Vriend. Fiery Arrow Collection. Leuven, Belgium: Peeters, 2000.

Catechism of the Catholic Church. Rev. ed., 1999. London: Burns & Oates, 2006.

Clapier, Jean. *Louis et Zélie Martin: Une sainteté pour tous les temps*. Paris: Presses de la Renaissance, un département d'Édi8, 2009.

De Meester, Conrad, ed. *I Have Found God: Complete Works of Elizabeth of the Trinity*. Vol. 2, *Letters from Carmel*. Translated by Anne Englund Nash. Washington, D.C.: ICS Publications, 1995.

Francis, Pope. *Amoris Laetitia: Apostolic Exhortation on Love in the Family*. London: St. Pauls, 2016.

Görres, Ida. *The Hidden Face*. San Francisco: Ignatius Press, 2003.

Guite, Malcolm. *Parable and Paradox: Sonnets on the Sayings of Jesus and Other Poems*. Norwich, UK: Canterbury, 2016.

"The Heart of the Deepest Truth." World Bishops' Message to Families, Rome, October 25, 1980.

Hénault-Morel, Thierry. *Louis et Zélie Martin*. Paris: Les Éditions du Cerf, 2015.

John of the Cross. *The Collected Works of St. John of the Cross*. Translated by Kieran Kavanaugh and Otilio Rodriguez. Washington D.C.: ICS Publications, 1991.

John Paul II. *On the Dignity and Vocation of Women (Mulieris Dignitatem)*. Apostolic letter. Vatican translation. Boston: Pauline Books, 1988.

———. *On the Role of the Christian Family in the Modern World (Familiaris Consortio)*. Apostolic exhortation. London: Catholic Truth Society, 1981.

Martin, Céline. *The Father of the Little Flower*. Translated by Michael Collins. Charlotte, N.C.: TAN Books, 2005. First published in 1955.

———. *The Mother of the Little Flower*. Translated by Michael Collins. Charlotte, N.C.: TAN Books, 2005. First published in 1955.

Mongin, Hélène. *The Extraordinary Parents of St. Thérèse of Lisieux*. Translated by Marsha Daigle-Williamson. Paris: Our Sunday Visitor, 2015.

Moorcroft, Jennifer. *Saint Thérèse of Lisieux and her Sisters*. Leominster, UK: Gracewing, 2014.

Piat, Stéphane-Joseph. *The Story of a Family: The Home of St. Thérèse of Lisieux*. Translated by a Benedictine of Stanbrook Abbey. Charlotte, N.C.: TAN Books, 2015. First English translation published as *The Story of a Family: The Home of the Little Flower*. New York: P.J. Kennedy and Sons, 1948.

Redmond, Paulinus. *Louis and Zélie Martin: The Seed and the Root of the Little Flower*. London: Quiller, 1995.

Renda, Frances, ed. *A Call to a Deeper Love: The Family Correspondence of the Parents of Saint Thérèse of the Child Jesus, 1863–1885*. Translated by Ann Connors Hess. New York: Society of St. Paul, 2011.

Schoen, Mary Kay. "Vowed to This Life." *America: The Jesuit Review*, September 19, 2011.

Singh, Kathleen Dowling. *The Grace in Dying*. New York: Harper One, 2000.

Six, Jean-François. *La véritable enfance de Thérèse de Lisieux*. Paris: Éditions du Seuil, 1971.

Stein, Edith. *The Hidden Life*. Edited by L. Gelber and Michael Linssen. Translated by Waltraut Stein. Washington, D.C.: ICS Publications, 1992.

Taylor, Therese. "Purgatory on Earth." *Social History of Medicine* 11, no. 3 (1998): 381–402.

Teresa of Avila. *The Collected Works of St. Teresa of Avila*. Translated by Kieran Kavanaugh and Otilio Rodriguez. Washington, D.C.: ICS Publications, 2012.

Thérèse of Lisieux. *Story of a Soul: The Autobiography of St. Thérèse of Lisieux*. Translated by John Clarke. 3rd ed. Washington, D.C.: ICS Publications, 1996.

Thomas à Kempis. *Imitation of Christ*. New York: Alba House, 1995.

Vatican Council II. *Apostolicam Actuositatem* (Decree on the Apostolate of the Laity). In *Vatican Council II: The Conciliar and Post Conciliar Documents*, edited by Austin Flannery. 2nd ed. Dublin: Dominican Publications, 1981.

———. *Lumen Gentium* (Dogmatic Constitution on the Church). London: Catholic Truth Society, 1965.

INDEX

A

abbreviations, xix–xxi
American War of Independence, 33, 36–37
Amoris Laetitia (The Joy of Love) (Pope Francis), 53, 75–76, 79, 137, 183, 192, 194
anticlericalism, 39–40
advice column, problems for, 14–15
Apostolicam Actuositatem (Decree on the Apostolate of the Laity) (Pope St. Paul VI), 182
archbishop of Paris, 35, 37, 39
Archconfraternity of Christian Mothers, 46, 189
The Ascent of Mount Carmel (St. John of the Cross), 161
Association of the Immaculate Heart of Mary, 41, 42
Augustinus (Jansen), 43–44

B

Barbadette, Joseph and Eugene, 41
Benedictine Order, 40
bereavement. *see* death and loss

Bloody Week (May 21–28, 1871), 39
Bohard, François, 27
Bon Sauveur Hospital, Caen, 168–73, 175
bookkeeping piety, 6, 45–46
Boureau, Fanie. *see* Martin, Fanie Boureau
breast cancer. *see* terminal illness

C

cancer. *see* terminal illness
Carmelite monastery, Lisieux
  Marie at, 135, 157, 200
  Pauline at, 134, 157, 190, 200
  Thérèse at, 150, 158, 163, 166–67, 200
Catholic Church
  anticlericalism and, 39–40
  as beleaguered, 46–47
  Jansenism, 43–46
  lay organizations, 46–47, 73, 146, 189
  our Lady, apparitions of, 34, 35, 40–43
  persecution of (1901–1905), 35, 40

reawakening, 46–47, 146–47
role in parenthood, 59
Catholic Circle, 48, 146
celibacy
church teaching on, 51–52
Louis's beliefs concerning, 30,
32, 52, 54
Charles, Father, 41, 42
Charles X, King, 34
Chartres, France, 147
childlessness, 56–57
children and childhood. *see also*
death and loss; parenting
discovery of identity, 20
family expectations for,
19–20
holiness through, 10
learning about love, 7
learning from experience,
5–6
"problem" children, 123–30,
136–38, 187, 199
questions for reflection, 32,
81, 119
strengthening parents,
121–32
communication, in marriage, 79
Communion, 44
contrition, 44
Costard, Marie Adélaïde, Sister,
170, 172, 175
Counsels to a Religious (John of
the Cross), 84
crises, challenge of, 79

D
Daughters of Charity, 25, 38,
40–41, 54
death and loss. *see also* terminal
illness
bereavement, 71–74, 149
of children, 64, 73–74
of Martin children, 62–63,
66–69, 71–72, 76
miscarriage, 72, 72n9, 81
reality of, 70–74
stillbirth, 63, 72–73, 72n8,
81
Decree on the Apostolate of the
Laity (*Apostolicam Actuositatem*) (Pope St. Paul VI), 182
dementia (Louis's), 161–77
behavioral changes, 164–67
crisis point, 167–68
as end or beginning?,
175–76
faith in God, 170–72,
175–76
family support, 1, 161,
172–73, 175, 176
hospitalization, 168–73, 175
humiliation, 170–72
last months, 173–74
onset, 159, 161, 162
prelude, 162–64
questions for reflection, 177
divorce statistics, 13
Doctrine of the Immaculate
Conception, 34, 42

E

Elizabeth of the Trinity, St., 97,
109, 109n7, 117, 185–86
Eucharist, 44, 182, 186–87
evangelical counsels, 53

F

Familiaris Consortio (On the
Role of the Christian Family
in the Modern World) (Pope
St. John Paul II), 180, 191, 192
family
caring ethos, 1, 116
challenges, 1–8
as domestic church, 191–92
God as integral part of, 6–7
mission of, 179–81
questions for reflection, 32
"sandwich generation," 75–76
support during terminal
illness, 116
fatherhood. *see* parenting
fears, 100, 117, 127–30
Ferry, Jules, 35, 39–40
First Empire, 33, 37
First Republic, 33, 37
fragmentation, feelings of,
196–97
France. *see* political and social
events
Francis, Pope, 53, 75–76, 79,
137, 183, 192, 194
Franco-Prussian War (1870–
1871), 35, 38, 41, 90, 155–56

French Revolution (1789), 22,
27, 33, 37
French revolution (1848), 34, 37

G

God
as integral part of family life,
7–8, 18
as judgmental, 44, 45–46, 49,
77–78
in Martin family motto, 141
as merciful, 45, 49
nurturing presence, 78
as Potter, 63–64, 79
presence during chronic
illness, 117
as stonemason, 84
Great St. Bernard hospice,
Switzerland, 28–29
Guérin, Céline (Zélie's
sister-in-law)
care for Martin children, 132,
134, 149–50, 173
inheritance, 91
Louis's dementia and, 173
Marie's correspondence, 114
Martin family move to
Lisieux and, 132
pregnancies, 64
stillborn son, 63, 72–73
Zélie on gifts for children, 187
Zélie on household help, 89
Zélie on Prussian occupation,
156

Zélie on suffering, 99
Zélie's breast cancer, 103–7, 112
Zélie's death and, 132
Zélie's father's death, 46
Zélie's sympathy for loss of
    pharmacy, 78
Guérin, Élise (Zélie's sister)
    childhood, 23–24, 25
    death, 63
    lay organizations, 46
    relationship with Zélie, 20,
        54–55, 71–72, 143
    tuberculosis, 74
    Visitation convent, 26, 40,
        54–55
    on Zélie's parenting philoso-
        phy, 128
Guérin, Guillaume (Zélie's
    great-uncle), 22, 33, 37
Guérin, Isidore (Zélie's brother)
    care for Martin children, 134,
        149–50, 172, 173
    character traits, 149–50
    childhood, 20, 23, 24
    Louis in Zélie's correspon-
        dence, 143
    Louis's dementia and, 165,
        167–68, 171–74, 176
    Louis's healthcare, 163
    Martin family move to
        Lisieux and, 132–33
    move to Lisieux, 74
    pharmacy business, 78, 87, 91,
        109–10, 124

political and church career, 91
stillborn son, 73
studying medicine in Paris, 43
Zélie on death of Hélène, 71
Zélie on evils of Paris, 29, 99
Zélie on her children, 58,
    59–60
Zélie on her writing skills, 24
Zélie on honoring Mary the
    Mother of God, 43
Zélie on marriage, 142
Zélie on suffering, 99
Zélie on their father, 94
Zélie on wet nurses, 65, 66
Zélie's breast cancer, 100, 103,
    104, 105, 114–15
Zélie's foundation of faith, 181
Zélie's last letter, 114
Zélie's loans to, 91–92
Guérin, Isidore (Zélie's father)
    birth, 33, 37
    death, 46, 63, 76
    later life, 75, 94
    military career, 23, 34, 37,
        38, 76
    retirement life, 23–24, 25
    with Zélie's family, 23, 75, 76
Guérin, Jeanne (niece), 63, 133
Guérin, Louise-Jeanne Macé
    (Zélie's mother), 23, 24–25,
    33, 46, 62
Guérin, Marie (niece), 63, 124,
    133, 174
Guérin, Paul (nephew), 63

guilt, 71
Guite, Malcolm, 178, 194

H
Halsted, William, 105n3
historical events. *see* political and
    social events
holiness, through marriage and
    children, 10

I
The Imitation of Christ (Thomas
    à Kempis), 148
Industrial Revolution, 38, 42,
    47–48
infertility, 56–57
The Interior Castle (Teresa of
    Ávila), 17, 145–46

J
Jansen, Cornelius, 43–44
Jansenism, 43–46, 77–78, 99
Jesuits, 44, 190
Jesus, 178, 179, 196–97
Joan of Arc, 141
Job, 60
John (of Revelation), 11
John of the Cross, St., 17, 51, 80,
    84, 161
John Paul II, Pope St., 121–22,
    180, 191, 192

"Josephite marriage," 52
The Joy of Love (*Amoris
    Laetitia*) (Pope Francis), 53,
    75–76, 79, 137, 183, 192, 194
July Monarchy, 34, 37
July Revolution, 34, 37, 40–41

L
Labouré, Catherine, 40–41, 42
La Salette, France, 41, 42, 46
Law of Separation of the
    Churches and the State
    (1905), 35
limbo, 46
Louis-Philippe, King, 34, 37,
    40–41
Louis XIII, King, 41
Louis XIV, King, 27n4
Louis XVIII, King, 27n4, 34
Lourdes, pilgrimages to, 43, 46,
    47, 99, 108, 111–13, 147

M
Macé, Louise-Jeanne. *see* Guérin,
    Louise-Jeanne Macé
Marais, Louise (household
    maid)
    burning letters, 187
    Léonie and, 107, 108n5,
        126–27
    Marie and, 69
    as psychologically abusive,
        107, 108n5, 126–27, 128

treated as family, 88–89
Zélie's charitable service, 92
marriage
    balance from husband, 31–32
    celibacy and virginity, 51–56
    challenge, growth through,
        1–8, 61, 79–81
    communication and rapport,
        79, 142–43
    creative energy, 189–92
    date of Martin marriage, 9,
        30, 35
    detours before we find
        ourselves, 50–54
    discovery and growth, 16–18
    Eucharist, 186–87
    family as domestic church,
        191–92
    family's mission, 179–81
    finding their way, 54–57
    God's transformation of
        suffering, 193–94
    honed by circumstances,
        15–16
    ideal marriage, notions of,
        50–61
    infertility, 56–57
    Louis's experience, 140–49
    Martin marriage, review of,
        197–200
    Martin marriage as example,
        15–17, 197–201
    mission of today, 201–2
    mustard seed parable, 178, 179

    as mutually enhancing
        partnership, 15
    necessary adjustments to,
        52–53
    paradox of marriage, 193–95
    power of prayer, 182–89
    prayer of the church, 182–86
    premarital adaptations to life
        and, 21–22, 26, 61
    questions for reflection, 18,
        61, 195, 202
    sacramentality, 10–11,
        13–14, 18, 183
    saints for today, 194–95
    searching for perfection,
        50–51
    self-discovery in, 30–32
    sequence of transitions,
        54–56
    spirituality of, 49, 178–95
    statistics, 13
    Sundays: daring to be differ-
        ent, 188–89
    support for one another, 116,
        141–42
    support from others, 181–82
    Vatican II, 53
    vocational guidance, 190–91
    when things go wrong, 60–61
    Zélie's dilemma, 54
    Zélie's happiness with, 59
Martin, Adolph (Louis's
    nephew), 27, 89, 191
Martin, Céline (daughter)

artistic talent, 164, 165–66
at Benedictine school in
  Lisieux, 133
birth, 63, 68
Carmel, call to, 164, 166
childhood, 77, 135, 151, 171,
  186
childhood nicknames, 154–55
health problems, 69, 74
on her father, 145, 148,
  149–50, 157, 182
in Lisieux, 133
Louis's death and, 174
Louis's dementia and,
  164–66, 167, 170,
  172–74, 175
photographs by, 16
pilgrimage to Rome, 158–59,
  163
Thérèse and, 77, 135, 171,
  186
wet nurse, 68–69, 101
Zélie's concerns about,
  130–31
Zélie's death and, 132
Zélie's impact on, 191
Zélie's pilgrimage to Lourdes,
  112
Martin, Fanie Boureau (Louis's
  mother)
arranging Louis and Zélie's
  marriage, 26, 30, 145, 179
death, 35
marriage, 27

Zélie's support for, 75
Martin, Fany (Louis's sister), 27,
  30
Martin, Hélène (daughter)
birth, 62, 124
childhood joy with siblings,
  68
death, 15, 63, 71, 72, 124
ear infection, 73
Louise Marais and, 126–27
wet nurse, 65–66
Martin, Joseph-Jean-Baptiste
  (son), 62, 63, 66, 67–68, 71, 76
Martin, Joseph-Louis (son), 62,
  66–67, 71, 76, 122–23
Martin, Léonie (daughter)
birth, 62
boarding school, 133
childhood joy with siblings,
  68
childhood nickname, 154
First Communion, 187
health problems, 74, 124,
  199
Louise Marais and, 126–27
Louis's dementia and,
  164–66, 167, 172, 173,
  175
move to Lisieux, 133
as "problem child," 123–30,
  137, 138, 187, 199
vocation, 129, 157–58, 173
Zélie's breast cancer and,
  107–8, 112–13, 129–30

Zélie's death and, 132

Martin, Louis. *see also* dementia;
marriage; parenting; work
and wealth
    bereavement at deaths of
        children, 71–72
    birth, 34
    bookkeeping piety, 6
    bravery and courage,
        155
    canonization, 1, 9, 11–13
    Catholic Circle, 48
    celibate life, as ideal, 30, 32,
        52, 54
    challenges faced by, 2–4
    childhood, 26–28
    as contemplative and solitary,
        15, 31, 32, 145–47
    correspondence with his
        children, 154–55
    correspondence with Zélie,
        21, 144
    crises deepening trust in God,
        60–61
    death, 35, 174
    epithelioma, 162–63
    failure at Latin, 21, 29
    fallacies about, 6, 141
    family heritage, 26–30,
        33–34, 37
    generosity, 92–93, 146, 156,
        182
    God as integral part of family
        life, 7, 141
    God's nurturing presence
        at darkest times, 78–81,
        170–71
    God's will as life focus, 49,
        51, 57
    as hardworking, 6
    heroism in everyday family
        life, 4–6
    impact of political and social
        events on, 35–36, 37–38,
        43, 46–49
    Jansenistic view, 77–78
    lay organizations, 46, 146
    leaving Paris for Alençon,
        34
    Léonie and, 124–25
    literary taste, 27, 28
    love of small things, 140–42
    love of the outdoors, 152–53,
        162–63, 174
    Mary the Mother of God
        statue, 43
    meeting Zélie on Alençon
        bridge, 30, 41
    monastic retreats, 189
    in Paris, 29, 37–38
    pilgrimages, 43, 47, 74,
        111–12, 124, 147,
        154–55, 158–59, 163
    prayer, 74, 77, 124, 129
    rejected as monk, 21, 28–29,
        52, 145
    religious devotions, 77,
        128–29, 163, 186

as "sandwich generation,"
75–76
vocations, 141, 175–76
watchmaking, love of small
things, 140–41
watchmaking, training and
apprenticeship, 28–29, 37
watchmaking shop, 37–38,
85, 93
watchmaking shop, sale of,
89–90, 144, 147
on Zélie dressing up children,
122–23
Zélie's breast cancer and, 100,
102, 104, 108, 111–13,
116
Zélie's death and, 149
Zélie's lacemaking business
and, 89–90, 111, 141,
147–49
Martin, Marie (daughter)
baptism, 64
birth, 62
care for younger siblings,
134–37
childhood, 58, 68, 186, 188
childhood nickname, 154,
155, 200
First Communion, 187
health problems, 74, 93–94,
131
Léonie and, 126–27
Memoirs, 66, 68
move to Lisieux, 133

Paris excursion, 154
siblings' wet nurses, 66, 69
Thérèse and, 131, 134–35,
137
vocation, 135, 157, 190, 200
Zélie's concerns about, 130
Zélie's death and, 114–15,
132
Zélie's pilgrimage to Lourdes,
112–13
Martin, Mélanie-Thérèse
(daughter), 63, 69, 71
Martin, Pauline (daughter)
birth, 62
care for younger siblings, 134,
135, 188
at Carmel, 134, 157, 190, 200
childhood, 58, 59–60, 65, 68
childhood nickname, 154,
155, 200
Léonie and, 125–26
Louise Marais and, 126–27
Louis's dementia and, 167–68
move to Lisieux, 133, 150
Paris excursion, 154
Zélie's breast cancer and,
107–8, 110
Zélie's correspondence, 14,
55, 80, 102, 122, 123, 130,
142–43
Zélie's death and, 132
Zélie's pilgrimage to Lourdes,
112–13
Zélie's prayer for, 122

Martin, Pierre-François (Louis's father), 27, 33, 37, 62, 75, 76
Martin, Thérèse (daughter)
    at Benedictine school in Lisieux, 133–34
    birth, 35, 63, 76
    at Carmel, 150, 158, 163, 166–67, 200
    childhood, as parenting challenge, 133–37
    childhood illness, 43, 134
    childhood nicknames, 154–55, 166, 200
    childhood relationship with siblings, 77, 131, 134–35, 137, 171, 186, 188
    childhood spirituality, 45, 186, 188
    "Christmas conversion," 135
    death, 35, 40
    on elevators, 38
    "Little Way," 141
    Louis's dementia and, 166–67, 171–72
    pilgrimage to Rome, 158–59, 163
    relationship with Louis, 133–37, 151, 154–55, 158, 163–64, 166–67
    wet nurse, 76–77
    Zélie's breast cancer and, 107
    Zélie's death and, 132, 135
    Zélie's impact on, 80, 92, 191
    Zélie's pilgrimage to Lourdes, 112

Martin, Zélie. see also marriage; parenting; terminal illness; work and wealth
    bereavement at deaths of children, 15, 69, 71–73
    birth, 34, 37
    bookkeeping piety, 6, 45–46
    canonization, 1, 9, 11–13
    caring ethos, 21, 75, 88–89, 94
    on Catholic Circle, 48
    challenges faced by, 2–4
    childhood, 14, 20–21, 23–25
    correspondence with brother, 14, 24, 29, 30, 58, 59–60, 65, 66, 71, 99, 100, 142, 143, 181
    correspondence with Louis, 21, 142, 144
    correspondence with Pauline, 55, 80, 125–26, 130, 142–43
    correspondence with sister-in-law, 30, 46, 64, 78, 104–7, 156
    crises deepening trust in God, 60–61
    on death, 14, 15, 75, 121
    death of, 35, 63, 114–15, 149
    determination and courage, 25, 30
    education, 24, 25
    energy and vibrancy, 6
    fallacies about, 6

family heritage, 22–26,
    33–34
generosity, 92–93
God as integral part of family
    life, 7, 12
God's nurturing presence at
    darkest times, 78–81
God's will as life focus, 49, 51,
    54, 56
handing herself over to God's
    care, 87, 102, 108–9
health, 21, 24
heroism in everyday family
    life, 4–6
impact of political and social
    events on, 35–36, 39, 43,
    45–49
Jansenism, influence of, 45
Jansenistic view, 45, 77–78
lacemaking, training in, 25,
    30, 54, 84–85
lacemaking business, challenges,
    60, 86–87, 88, 93–94
lacemaking business, found-
    ing of, 25–26
lacemaking business, Louis's
    support for, 89–90, 111,
    141
lacemaking business, success,
    48, 54, 88, 90, 92
lay organizations, 46–47, 73,
    189
Mary the Mother of God,
    importance of, 43, 110,
    123

meeting Louis on Alençon
    bridge, 30, 41
mourning death of her father,
    46, 76
prayer, 77, 122, 123, 129
rejected as nun, 25, 38, 52, 54
relationship with Élise
    (sister), 30, 54–55, 71–72
religious devotions, 77,
    128–29, 186–87
on sainthood, 45, 99, 102, 123
as "sandwich generation,"
    75–76
on suffering, 45–46, 98, 99,
    109
on Thérèse, 76–77
Third Order of Franciscans,
    189
on war as punishment, 45
wet nurses and, 48, 65–66
work ethic, 15, 25, 30
writing award, 24
Mary the Mother of God
    apparitions of, 34, 35, 40–43
    Thérèse's recovery from
        hallucinations, 43, 134
    Zélie's trust in, 43, 110, 123
Memoirs (Marie Martin), 66, 68
Miraculous Medal, 34, 40–41,
    42
miscarriage, 72, 72n9, 81
Missionaries of Our Lady of La
    Salette, 42
mission of family, 179–81
money. see wealth

motherhood. *see* parenting
Mulieris Dignitatem (On the
Dignity and Vocation of
Women) (Pope St. John Paul
II), 121–22
mustard seed parable, 178, 179

N

Napoleon, Prince Imperial, 26
Napoleon Bonaparte I, Emperor
(France), 33, 37, 155n18
Napoleon III, Emperor (France),
23, 26, 34, 38
Nocturnal Eucharistic Adora-
tion, 46, 146
Nogrix, Mr., 149
Notre-Dame de Victoires. *see*
Our Lady of Victories
Notta, Dr., 106, 116

O

On the Dignity and Vocation
of Women (*Mulieris Digni-
tatem*) (Pope St. John Paul
II), 121–22
On the Role of the Christian
Family in the Modern World
(*Familiaris Consortio*) (Pope
St. John Paul II), 180, 191, 192
original sin, 44
our Lady. *see* Mary the Mother
of God
Our Lady of La Salette, 34, 41

Our Lady of Lourdes, 34, 41,
42–43, 108
Our Lady of Pontmain, 35, 41
Our Lady of the Immaculate
Conception, 34, 42
Our Lady of the Miraculous
Medal, 34, 40–41, 42
Our Lady of Victories, 34, 41,
42, 43, 186

P

Parable and Paradox (Guite),
178, 194
parenting. *see also* children and
childhood
aiming for perfection, 57–58
as captain of the ship, 136
challenges, 2, 5, 58–59
children strengthen the
parents, 121–32
crises deepening trust in God,
60–61
deaths of children, 62–64,
66–69, 71–73
discipline, 153
dressing up children, 122–23
entertaining bored children,
131
experience of, 57–60
fears for the future, 127–30
financial security for children,
31, 88
First Communions, 187
guilt, 71

happy home for children, 31, 57, 122

healing pain of own childhood, 65

joys of, 59–60, 66–67

learning from troubled children, 136–38

Léonie as "problem child," 123–30, 137, 138, 187, 199

Léonie's sisters, 130–32

Louis's journey, 140–60

Martin family in Alençon, 121

Martin family move to Lisieux, 132–33

Martins as inspiration and example, 5, 58

mission accomplished, 157–59, 163–64, 200

parental failings, 6, 11, 12

playing and singing with children, 31, 60, 65, 134, 150–53

postpartum depression, 58–59

prayers, 122, 123

proud parents, 64–65

questions for reflection, 61, 138–39, 160

reality of, 63–69

role of the church, 59

sick children, 46, 94

single father, 132–36, 149–56

Thérèse as parenting challenge, 133–37

transforming experience of, 120–39

transition to, 58–59

"vocation," signs of, 129

wet nurses for Martin children, 65–71, 76–77, 101

when things go wrong, 60–61

wider world excursions, 153–55

Paris

archbishop, 35, 37, 39

excursions to, 38, 154

Franco-Prussian War, 38

Isidore Guérin in, 29, 43, 99

Louis in, 29, 37–38

Paris Commune, 35, 39

Paul, St., 11, 147, 193

Paul VI, Pope St., 182

perfect contrition, 44

perfection

all Christians called to, 53

marriage goals, 50–51

in modern family life, 53

parenthood goals, 57–58

though virginity or celibacy, 51–52

Pichon, Almire, Father, 190

Pius VI, Pope, 33, 37

Pius IX, Pope, 42

political and social events, 33–49

anticlericalism, 39–40
apparitions of our Lady, 34,
35, 40–43
beleaguered church, 46–47
church and state, 39–48
empires and republics, 36–39
First Empire, 33, 37
First Republic, 33, 37
Industrial Revolution, 38,
47–48
Jansenism, 43–46
Paris Commune, 35, 39
questions for reflection, 49
Second Empire, 34, 38
Second Republic, 34, 37–38
Third Republic, 35, 38
timeline, 33–35
Poor Clares, 47, 73, 129, 158,
189
prayer, in marriage, 182–89
the Eucharist, 186–87
prayer of the church, 182–86
Sundays: daring to be different, 188–89
predestination, 44
purgatory, 46

R
"The Rainbow" (Wordsworth),
140
Revolution of 1848, 34, 37
Roman Catholic Church. see
Catholic Church
Romet, Vital, 104, 106, 108n6

Roussel Law (1874), 70n6

S
saints
Martins as models, 200–201
as normal people, 51
perceived as spiritual super-
stars, 50–51
"sandwich generation," 75–76
Schoen, Mary Kay, poem by,
184–85
Second Empire, 34, 38
Second Republic, 34, 37–38
Second Solemn Communion,
187n6
Second Vatican Council
(1962–1965), 53
secularism, 39–40
Sedan, Battle of (1870), 38
self-discovery, in marriage,
30–32
Semallé, France, 66, 69
Sisters of Mercy, 114
Sisters of St. Vincent de Paul, 172
"Sketch of Mount Carmel" (St.
John of the Cross), 161
social events. see political and
social events
Soligny-la-Trappe, 189
Soubirous, Bernadette, 41,
42–43, 108
The Spiritual Canticle (John of
the Cross), 51, 80
St. Helena medal, 23, 38

stillbirth, 63, 72–73, 72n8, 81
St. Vincent de Paul Society, 182
suffering
    Jansenistic emphasis on, 60,
        77–78, 99, 109
    Martin family, 193
    as normal, 98
    as path to sanctity, 45–46
    transformation into deeper
        awareness, 193–94

T
Taillé, Rose, 66–67, 69, 76–77
teenagers, 5, 7. see also children
Teresa of Ávila, St., 17, 145–46
terminal illness (Zélie's breast
    cancer), 97–119
    beginnings, 98, 100–103
    denial, 103
    desire to be cured, 110–11
    diagnosis, 104–5
    facing illness and death,
        97–99
    family support, 116
    fear, 100
    God's presence, 108–9, 117,
        118
    informing the family, 107–8
    isolation, 101
    Jansenistic influences, 99
    last days, 111–15
    lessons from, 115–18
    Lourdes pilgrimage, 43, 99,
        108, 111–13

medical advice, 106–7
    openness about, 117–18
    pain, 113–14
    period of waiting, 102
    questions for reflection, 119
    reality of death, as pivotal
        point, 104–8
    resignation, 109–10
    review of life, 102
    stages of adjustment, 115–16
    surgical option, 100,
        104–6
    terminal care and death,
        114–15
    transformation, 108–11
Thérèse of Lisieux. see Martin,
    Thérèse
Third Order of Franciscans,
    46–47, 189
Third Republic, 35, 38
Thomas à Kempis, 148
Trappist monastery, 189

U
Urban VIII, Pope, 43

V
Vatican II, 53
virginity, church teaching on,
    51–52
Visitation Order, 26, 40, 158,
    173, 190
Vital Romet, 104, 106, 108n6
vocational guidance, 190–91

"Vowed to This Life" (Schoen),
    184–85

W

Waitley, Denis, 120
wealth of Martin family,
    90–94
    holiness and, 91–93
    questions for reflection,
        95–96
    sources of, 90–92, 148
    work-family tensions,
        93–94
wet nurses
    deaths of babies in care of,
        47–48, 66–67
    for factory-working mothers,
        47, 66n1, 70

for Martin children, 65–71,
    76–77, 101
neglect of charges, 68–69
regulations, 70n6
shortage of, 47
"white marriage," 52
Wordsworth, William, 140
work and wealth, 82–96. *see also*
    wealth of Martin family
    assumptions for sanctity, 84–86
    bricks and stitches of life,
        82–84
    dual-income family, 86–88
    household help, 88–90
    questions for reflection,
        95–96
    work, 82–90
World Bishops' Message to
    Families (1980), 191–92

About Us

ICS Publications, based in Washington, D.C., is the publishing house of the Institute of Carmelite Studies (ICS) and a ministry of the Discalced Carmelite Friars of the Washington Province (U.S.A.). The Institute of Carmelite Studies promotes research and publication in the field of Carmelite spirituality, especially about Carmelite saints and related topics. Its members are friars of the Washington Province.

Discalced Carmelites are a worldwide Roman Catholic religious order comprised of friars, nuns, and laity—men and women who are heirs to the teaching and way of life of Teresa of Ávila and John of the Cross, dedicated to contemplation and to ministry in the church and the world.

Information about their way of life is available through local diocesan vocation offices, or from the Discalced Carmelite Friars vocation directors at the following addresses:

Washington Province:
1525 Carmel Road, Hubertus, WI 53033

California-Arizona Province:
P.O. Box 3420, San Jose, CA 95156

Oklahoma Province:
5151 Marylake Drive, Little Rock, AR 72206

Visit our websites at:
www.icspublications.org   and   *http://ocdfriarsvocation.org*